T0328474

Cambridge Elements ≡

Elements in Eighteenth-Century Connections
edited by
Eve Tavor Bannet
University of Oklahoma
Rebecca Bullard
University of Reading

HOW AND WHY TO DO THINGS WITH EIGHTEENTH-CENTURY MANUSCRIPTS

Michelle Levy
Simon Fraser University
Betty A. Schellenberg
Simon Fraser University

CAMBRIDGE
UNIVERSITY PRESS

CAMBRIDGE
UNIVERSITY PRESS

University Printing House, Cambridge CB2 8BS, United Kingdom

One Liberty Plaza, 20th Floor, New York, NY 10006, USA

477 Williamstown Road, Port Melbourne, VIC 3207, Australia

314–321, 3rd Floor, Plot 3, Splendor Forum, Jasola District Centre,
New Delhi – 110025, India

103 Penang Road, #05–06/07, Visioncrest Commercial, Singapore 238467

Cambridge University Press is part of the University of Cambridge.

It furthers the University's mission by disseminating knowledge in the pursuit of education,
learning, and research at the highest international levels of excellence.

www.cambridge.org
Information on this title: www.cambridge.org/9781108926133
DOI: 10.1017/9781108921855

First published 2021

A catalogue record for this publication is available from the British Library.

ISBN 978-1-108-92613-3 Paperback
ISSN 2632-5578 (online)
ISSN 2632-556X (print)

How and Why to Do Things with Eighteenth-Century Manuscripts

Elements in Eighteenth-Century Connections

DOI: 10.1017/9781108921855
First published online: November 2021

Michelle Levy
Simon Fraser University

Betty A. Schellenberg
Simon Fraser University

Author for correspondence: Betty A. Schellenberg, Schellen@sfu.ca

Abstract: This Element examines eighteenth-century manuscript forms, their functions in the literary landscape of their time, and the challenges and practices of manuscript study today. Drawing on both literary studies and book history, Levy and Schellenberg offer a guide to the principal forms of literary activity carried out in handwritten manuscripts produced in the first era of print dominance, 1730–1820. After an opening survey of sociable literary culture and its manuscript forms, numerous case studies explore what can be learned from three manuscript types: the verse miscellany, the familiar correspondence, and manuscripts of literary works that were printed. A final section considers issues of manuscript remediation up to the present, focusing particularly on digital remediation. The Element concludes with a brief case study of the movement of Phillis Wheatley's poems between manuscript and print. This Element is also available as Open Access on Cambridge Core.

Keywords: correspondence, digital remediation, literary manuscripts, manuscript studies, social authorship

ISBNs: 9781108926133 (PB), 9781108921855 (OC)
ISSNs: 2632-5578 (online), 2632-556X (print)

Contents

Introduction

This Element focuses on eighteenth-century manuscript forms and their functions in the literary landscape of their time. Situated at the intersection of two fields, literary history and book history, the eighteenth-century manuscript, or handwritten document, has often been acknowledged in passing, but its ongoing production, circulation, and influence have only recently begun to be studied as significant phenomena in their own right.[1] One obvious reason for this neglect is the increasing dominance of the print medium as the century progressed. In particular, the emergence in the eighteenth century of widely distributed forms like the newspaper, magazine, and cheap reprint edition, as well as the development of circulating libraries and book societies, provided an opportunity for readers of modest means and in provincial settings to engage with literature, especially poetry, essays, and fiction, in print, and so that is where we tend to encounter these forms now, especially through digital facsimiles. However, often these new venues simply mirrored and amplified existing manuscript-based practices, and the arrival of cheap, mass-produced print with the invention of the steam press became a reality only after 1820. Thus, print has cast an artificially large shadow over what was in fact a well-established, lively, and accessible culture of manuscript production and circulation.

For the nineteenth and twentieth centuries, print was not only cheap, ubiquitous, and disposable: in new codex forms like the anthology, the multivolume series, and the encyclopedia, it had also become the medium of fixity and permanence, claiming to preserve the best of human thought and achievement. By contrast, from the perspective of the eighteenth-century participant in literary activities such as poetry reading and writing, the manuscript medium was the preferred way to preserve from destruction not only anti-government poetry recited in the coffeehouses or a birthday poem enclosed in a letter from a friend but also the verse account of a local scandal or a poem by Jonathan Swift that had been printed in regional newspapers.[2] That this confidence in script's potential for longevity could be well placed is confirmed by the many surviving literary manuscripts of the period, in multiple formats and genres, from collections of culinary and medicinal "receipts" to the working notebooks of Mary

---

[1] Important recent studies of eighteenth-century manuscript culture build on the work of scholars of Early Modern literature. In addition to our own recent contributions (Levy, *Literary Manuscript Culture* and *Family Authorship*; Schellenberg, "Eighteenth-Century Manuscript Verse Miscellanies" and *Literary Coteries*), extended arguments for the ongoing vigor of scribal practices in the long eighteenth century have been made by Margaret J. M. Ezell, *Social Authorship*; George Justice and Nathan Tinker, *Women's Writing*; David Allan, *Commonplace Books*; and Rachael Scarborough King, *Writing to the World* and *After Print*.

[2] McKitterick, *Print, Manuscript*, ch. 1, has detailed the slow development of print reliability in the period and the confidence placed in scribal activity as an alternative.

Shelley's *Frankenstein* (1818). This is not to suggest that the survival record is not mixed, as will be illustrated in this Element's Coda by the tragic fate of Phillis Wheatley's manuscript book of poems, sought by her husband after her death and now considered irrevocably lost, in contrast with the recent unexpected recovery of her first poem in the diary of the Rev. Jeremy Belknap.

The accessibility of eighteenth-century manuscripts today is a more complicated question, as they are deposited in various archives and often available only to viewers with specialist credentials. Because all manuscripts are unique copies, they invite attention not only to survival but also to issues of remediation, that is, how they have been reproduced in different media, whether through various types of photographic reproduction or typographical representation in print editions. Even works that were printed in their own day generally come to us in remediated forms, but familiarity with the conventions of print-based remediation can blind us to the framing and potentially distorting effects of a typeset, edited, and annotated modern print edition of, for example, Thomas Gray's *Elegy Written in a Country Churchyard*, as opposed to either the personal correspondence in which early drafts of the poem were shared or the six-penny pamphlet first published by Robert Dodsley in 1751.

As Mark Bland contends, "manuscripts are always witnesses to something other than the texts they preserve";[3] in this Element, we are interested in the stories they have to tell about their creation, function, survival history, and ongoing importance. Above all, this Element aims to add to our growing recognition of the vigor of social and scribal modes of circulation in what has often been assumed to be the historical moment of print saturation. Looking at past centuries of print dominance, we explore a period when manuscript production was widely practiced and thriving in an interdependent relation with print – when, in fact, print had afforded new importance and variety to a range of manuscript practices.[4] We offer a guide to principal forms of literary activity carried out in handwritten manuscript forms in the eighteenth century (from the 1730s to the 1820s), beginning with an introductory section surveying the media landscape of the period from the perspective of manuscripts. The following three sections look in turn at what literary scholars can learn from three manuscript types: verse miscellanies as a distinctive manuscript genre; the familiar correspondence as an extended, collaborative text; and manuscripts of literary works that were printed early in their life cycle. These three "case study" sections are followed by a discussion of manuscript remediations from the nineteenth century to the present, focusing particularly on digital remediation.

---

[3] Bland, *Guide*, p. 9.

[4] Scholarship demonstrating the particular importance of scribal circulation for women is summarized in Levy, "Women and the Book."

A final case study of the uneven movement of Wheatley's poems between manuscript and print epitomizes the interpenetration of these media in the eighteenth century, as well as what manuscripts have to teach us now. While this Element has been conceived and developed as a joint endeavor, readers familiar with our work will recognize Schellenberg's interests in the first two case studies, with the latter sections on authorial manuscripts and their remediations drawing on Levy's expertise. Throughout this collaborative Element, we jointly aim not only to familiarize the reader with eighteenth-century manuscript culture but also to make clear the practices, challenges, and potential of manuscript study in the twenty-first century.

1 Manuscript Culture and Social Authorship in the Eighteenth Century

As noted in our introduction, manuscripts can be seen as "witnesses" to human activity, to the motivations, processes, and cultural contexts that produced them. Such an approach views the manuscript as a material object rather than simply a "text." In the words of Jerome McGann, "documents are far from self-transparent. They are riven with the multiple histories of their own making."[5] In addition to these histories, manuscripts also tell us about how they were used, shared, and saved. By studying manuscripts, we can learn about a range of activities first identified by Early Modern scholars as "manuscript culture" or "the manuscript system," with characteristic practices distinct from, but still operating in tandem with, those of the world of print production.[6] Writing within this culture is sometimes described as "social authorship":[7] manuscripts were produced, read, revised, circulated, and preserved in the context of social networks, whether held together by ties of kinship, patronage, or more egalitarian friendship – and most often, some combination of all three.

Donald H. Reiman's threefold taxonomy of manuscripts created since the arrival of print technology is helpful here. Between the categories of private manuscript – intended for the author or only a very select few – and public manuscript – designed expressly for a large, indiscriminate, often print-based audience – lies a third category, the confidential manuscript, addressed to a social readership.[8] It is this latter category of confidential manuscript, used to create and sustain social bonds, that is central to manuscript culture in the

---

[5] McGann, *Republic*, p. 45.

[6] Influential descriptions of this manuscript culture can be found in Hobbs, *Early Seventeenth-Century Verse Miscellany Manuscripts*; Marotti, *Manuscript, Print, and the English Renaissance Lyric*, ch. 1; Beal, "Notions in Garrison" and *Dictionary*. For a very recent practical guide to manuscript studies, see James, *English Paleography and Manuscript Culture, 1500–1800*.

[7] Ezell, *Social Authorship*.   [8] Reiman, *Modern Manuscripts*, pp. 10–17.

eighteenth century. Parents wrote letters to children at school, households kept books of culinary and medical "receipts" from generation to generation; networks of women and men exchanged texts about matters ranging from religion to education to politics. Created within household libraries, schools, and clubs, literary texts were just one manuscript type among many, drafted and exchanged in notebooks and on loose sheets, sent through the postal system, copied into commonplace books and albums, and at times submitted to (or obtained clandestinely by) periodical editors or booksellers for printing in magazines or as separate pamphlets. Sometimes these works were circulated in advance of print publication; sometimes they were simply shared for enjoyment without any plan for printing them – even though a widely circulated manuscript could become "public" in its own right and would likely eventually end up in the hands of a printer.

Before moving to a description of manuscript forms, we pause to define a key term and to further explain the Element's scope. We use the terms "publication" and "publish" to refer to print dissemination. The hand copying of texts as a commercial trade in the seventeenth century has been called "scribal publication,"[9] but the scribal profession in Britain declined considerably after 1700 (though this is less true for the American colonies and Ireland), and the copying we consider in this Element was neither centralized nor remunerated. "Publication" in this Element therefore refers to the act of publicly printing a work for distribution and, usually, sale. We confine our discussion to literary manuscripts, by which we mean manuscripts that contain recognizable literary genres – for this period, primarily poetry, fiction, and familiar letters. Although we exclude from consideration a number of genres that are not usually considered literary, such as business records and recipes, and literary forms such as drama, sermons, and essays that do not appear among our examples, this is not because any of these forms are unimportant or irrelevant to a history of the circulation of handwritten documents. Rather, we have chosen to focus on those literary genres that had significant manuscript circulation (including the travel narrative, which we will see embedded within the familiar letter) and that therefore the literary scholar will wish to take into account.

1.1 Manuscript Formats

While a unit of manuscript material – for example, a single sheet of paper with handwriting on it – may coincide with a complete "text" or "work" if that single sheet contains a complete copy, say, of Hester Chapone's widely circulated "Ode. Occasion'd by Reading Sonnets in the Style and Manner of Spenser" and

---

[9] Love, *Scribal Publication.*

no other work, that is often not the case. A manuscript in the material sense – that single, handwritten sheet – may give physical form either to multiple texts (if it contains three or four of Chapone's odes) or to a partial text only (if it contains only the first two stanzas of Chapone's "Ode. Occasion'd by Reading Sonnets"). In the sections that follow, when we speak of the manuscript of a work, we will generally be discussing the complete work, such as Thomas Gray's 1751 poem *An Elegy Written in a Country Churchyard* or a letter from the Bluestocking Elizabeth Montagu to her friend Anne Donnellan, whether the text is inscribed onto a folded sheet of paper (termed a manuscript "separate") or written into a bound notebook. However, since the material state in which a manuscript work was brought into being, circulated, and preserved is often pertinent to our interpretation of its meaning and social function – its "multiple histories" – we will frequently look to its material form to guide us in studying it. Two small holes in the top corners of a letter manuscript signal that a pin was once used to bundle it together with others for subsequent reference and therefore that it was considered important in its own time. Similarly, the small size of Jane Austen's handmade notebooks reportedly allowed her to hide her novel manuscripts when visitors entered the room. Although we attempt to distinguish clearly between these two meanings of the term "manuscript" – the handwritten version of a literary work like *Frankenstein* and the many note-books filled in drafting and preparing it for printing – the reader of this study must bear the distinction in mind.

It is therefore helpful to devote some time to a preliminary discussion of manuscript formats and how these, in some cases, correlate with certain literary genres. Virtually all eighteenth-century manuscripts are made of the same material: rag paper, made from salvaged textiles. Blank writing paper could be purchased, generally from a stationer's shop, in different formats, but most commonly as sheets of various sizes and qualities, with the finest white paper the most expensive. Although recent research has emphasized the relative affordability of single sheets of paper,[10] writers who used a great deal of it showed their awareness of its cost and what that costliness signified. The early eighteenth-century poet Alexander Pope, for example, is notorious for having drafted his translation of *The Iliad* on the backs of letters from his friends (Figure 1), as well as for having the prestigious and costly subscription volumes of his translation of Homer's *Iliad* printed on "royal paper" (one of the largest sizes of paper for printing; 59.5 × 47 cm/23.5 × 18.5 in.) with an abundance of white space to set off the print.

---

[10] Wolfe, "Was Early Modern Writing Paper Expensive?"

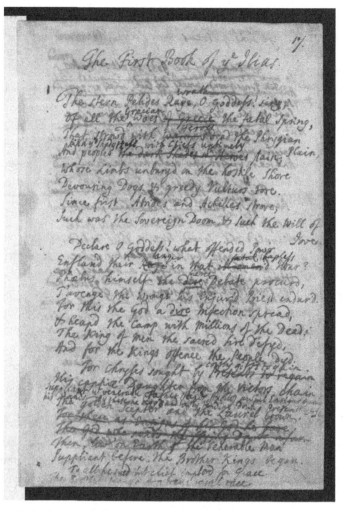

Figure 1 A draft page of Alexander Pope's manuscript of *The Iliad,* written on the verso of a letter to his friend John Caryll. BL MS Add. MS 4807, The British Library.

Loose sheets (also referred to as "leaves" of paper) were used for letter writing. To prepare a letter, a rectangular sheet of paper would be folded in half crosswise. This would create a two-leaf pamphlet (a bifolium), with four pages for writing. Typically, the writer would fill up to the first three pages, leaving the fourth blank or mostly blank. Folding this quarto sheet four more times created a tidy packet, which was sealed (usually with wax), leaving what remained visible of the blank fourth page to be inscribed with the address (Figure 2). Before the eighteenth century, the exchange of handwritten letters had long been an essential practice among the powerful and socially elite who

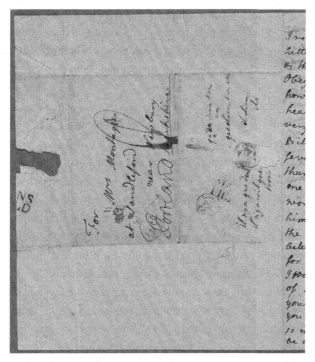

Figure 2 The address-bearing page of a letter from the Duchess of Portland to Elizabeth Montagu, 24 August 1747, mo227, p. 4, Montagu Collection, The Huntington Library.

had political news to convey, alliances to negotiate, and far-flung family relations to maintain. Such exchanges, however, required not only relatively sophisticated skills in literacy and handwriting (and, often, the services of one or more secretaries) but also material tools – paper, quill pens, ink, sealing wax, blotting sand ("pounce"), and so on – and, above all, the means to procure or take advantage of state or private messenger services to convey written letters safely over long and sometimes perilous distances.[11] With the development of a London-centered postal service available to the public in the later seventeenth century, the founding of the Penny Post efficiently crisscrossing the city, and significant improvements to the national network of postal routes in the first half of the eighteenth century, the "familiar letter" genre became a widely cultivated form adapted to the everyday business, social, and personal needs of a very broad spectrum of the population, making this the golden age of letter writing.

---

[11] For a detailed account of letter production, circulation, and preservation that precedes the public postal service but remains very applicable to eighteenth-century practices, see Daybell, *Material Letter*.

A solid grounding in the conventions of what Susan E. Whyman has called "epistolary literacy" offered the means to professional and social advancement and enabled an increasingly mobile population to maintain familial and business ties over great distances, including those between Britain and its colonies.[12]

As James Daybell has noted, "the material rhetorics of the manuscript page were central to the ways in which letters communicated"; this included such physical characteristics as size and quality of paper, formatting and wording of the sign-off, amount of blank space, and type and color of the seal. Yet, in what is often called the "Republic of Letters" – that is, the sphere of wide-ranging intellectual inquiry in which the most literate individuals of European states and their colonies participated – correspondence could become more: it allowed for in-depth and extended exchanges, often spanning decades and adapting to frequent relocations, on subjects of shared literary, historical, moral, and philosophical interest. Members of sociable literary networks circulated manuscript poetry or other short texts through enclosures in letters; letters also conveyed in return the constructive criticism that their authors sought.[13] More generally, a well-written familiar letter was in itself a literary creation, offering verbal wit, clever allusions, sententious wisdom, and moral commentary for the entertainment and improvement of its readers. While the letters of celebrated print-based authors "were increasingly used to construct authorial identity,"[14] both in their lifetimes and posthumously, epistolary talent in itself could form the basis of a literary reputation, and the letters of Elizabeth Montagu, as discussed in Section 3, were copied and circulated among her correspondents from the time she was in her twenties.

Loose sheets were also used in a variety of other ways: to compose an occasional poem (verses written to mark a particular occasion, such as a friend's birthday or the death of an infant) for enclosure in a letter, for example; to record a sermon; or to record a poem that had been read in a book borrowed from an acquaintance or from a subscription or circulating library. Collections of these manuscript separates could be hand-sewn, pasted, or professionally bound into books, enhancing their chances of survival. More simply, multiple loose sheets could also be folded and placed into quires (sheets of paper folded once with folds placed together to create a booklet). Increasingly in the eighteenth

---

[12] Whyman, *The Pen and the People*. King, *Writing to the World*, explores the letter as a "bridge genre" that becomes the formal foundation of numerous print genres. Eve Tavor Bannet, *Empire of Letters*, details the dependence of eighteenth-century transatlantic business and social relations on a highly developed culture of letter writing.

[13] Paul Trolander and Zeynep Tenger, *Sociable Criticism*.

[14] Curran, *Samuel Richardson*, p. 3; Curran's is the fullest case study to date of a published author developing his own epistolary style and identity as part of this phenomenon.

century what we call notebooks – prebound blank paper-books – were purchased from stationers, as in the case of Sarah Wilmot's and Dorothy Wordsworth's books, discussed in Sections 2 and 4, respectively. Such prebound books might be of various sizes and qualities, sometimes with ruled margins and even ruled lines, with the smaller, simpler ones often covered only with a sheet of marbled paper and the quartos with stiffened cardboard covers (Figure 3). Among the most common manuscript genres for which stationers' paper-books were used were commonplace books – organized collections of memorable or edifying quotations; miscellanies – collections, usually of poems, often sourced from print; scrapbooks – compilations of printed and manuscript materials as well as, often, watercolor sketches, fabric, pressed flowers, and so on; and albums – collections of solicited poems or other handmade items. As access to print increased and literary fashions changed through the long eighteenth century, these forms succeeded one another in general popularity, with scrapbooks and albums coming to the fore in the 1820s. However, many notebooks defy any single categorization, as they were often what Margaret J. M. Ezell has described as "messy," "combin[ing] accounts of rents collected with copies of verses, alphabet exercises with prayers and diary entries."[15]

(a)   (b)

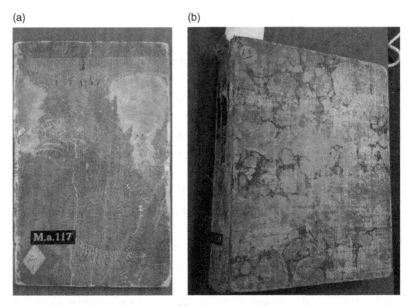

Figure 3 Notebooks covered with marbled paper and in the second case also with stiffened boards (Folger MS M.a.117 and M.a. 160).

---

[15] Ezell goes on to note that such books are "at present … largely invisible in studies of book history" (Ezell, "Invisible Books," p. 55).

For literary authors, as already noted, loose sheets were often used for enclosure of a work in a letter. The poet William Shenstone on several occasions writes to friends in an attempt to retrieve draft poems written on loose sheets that he has circulated for comment and then lost track of. In the case of a body of work or a longer work, handmade or purchased notebooks were useful for drafting, copying, and revising before the work's wider circulation among manuscript readers or its submission to a bookseller for printing. Thus Elizabeth Montagu's correspondence in the Huntington Library includes a folded booklet, held together by two small pins, of Hester Chapone's poems, seemingly used to interest Bluestocking friends and influencers like George Lyttelton in Chapone's work before she ventured into print. Some poets, such as Anne Finch, created volumes of their poetry in manuscript as an alternative to print; in Finch's case, many of her currently most well-known poems remained unprinted until the twentieth century. Whether destined for confidential manuscript circulation or for setting into type for printing, such "fair copies," unlike Shenstone's working drafts of poems sent to friends for feedback, were carefully produced by the author or an amanuensis to maximize correctness and legibility.

1.2 Intermediality

If texts could take on multiple manuscript forms in the long eighteenth century, it is not surprising that they also moved back and forth between media. Poetry, in particular, inhabited a media ecosystem wherein script and print were closely intertwined. Poetry is the literary genre that appears to have circulated most widely in manuscript form in this period, alongside other popular forms such as epitaphs and riddles, both of which were often rhymed verses. The poems most likely to circulate in this way were short and could easily be copied and exchanged. Many were the kinds of occasional verse already described: highly social in nature; addressed to members of one's social network as a means of sustaining personal relationships; and potentially copied, shared, or collected by others in the network or beyond who had gained access to the manuscripts. Other popular subgenres were topical satires, devotional lyrics, and courtship poems, all of which were of wide relevance or easily transferable to new contexts. When such a poem was submitted to a magazine or printed by a bookseller, it might achieve further circulation to a new audience. Since copying from print was also widespread, print publication of a poem did not prevent but rather stimulated more handwritten copying. Many poems were published in cheap miscellanies, short-lived periodicals, and regional news-papers; making a copy by hand could in these cases assist in the poem's preservation and transmission. Poetry of course was also published in more substantial book forms, but such books were costly, leading to even more copying by those who could not afford the purchase.

This extensive hand copying from print demonstrates that even after a poem had been published, manuscript circulation continued. Access and cost aside, copying could fill different needs than did possessing a printed version of a poem. The act of copying could involve copyists in creative activity, in the form of textual amendment (for example, readdressing a poem to a friend), arrangement in the company of other poems, and extra illustration (embellishment of a text through the addition of drawings, engravings, or other contextualizing materials). In the case of a very popular poem like Thomas Gray's *Elegy*, discussed in Section 4, copying the poem by hand into a verse miscellany absorbed the poem into a personally curated collection; arranging, revising, illustrating, and/or reciting the poem made it one's own.[16] And for a stylistically distinctive poem like the *Elegy*, making the poem one's own often included copying or creating a parody of it as well.

Such forms of manuscript circulation occurred as a result of a text's becoming public and therefore the object of widespread access. The latter half of the eighteenth century also saw printed pages become a kind of precursor to manuscript writing during the processes of literary production. Whereas in the early decades of the century, a press's compositors generally had free rein over accidentals such as punctuation, by mid-century printers and booksellers increasingly involved authors in correcting the proofs of their works before they were published. In the case of Laurence Sterne's 1765 novel *A Sentimental Journey*, we will see in Section 4 evidence of this developing tendency, though by no means a universal one. Given the limits of type and other equipment, a compositor would set a few sheets at a time, have these printed as proof sheets for correction, then solicit the author (or her agent) to make changes for the press workers to print, before proceeding to set the next section of the manuscript. The result was a print-manuscript hybrid that represented a collaboration between the compositor who had remediated the author's manuscript into printed proofs and the author/agent who in turn remediated that proof into a marked-up manuscript for reprinting. In such cases, we can use an author's manuscripts not necessarily to establish an authoritative text for a work but to learn more about the intermedial process of its composition.

Markings on manuscripts can also reveal a less congenial movement through the publication process. In the case of Anna Letitia Barbauld's 1804 edition of

---

[16] Colclough, *Consuming Texts*, chs. 2 and 3; Allan, *Commonplace Books*, chs. 10 and 11; Williams, *Social Life*, ch. 5.

novelist Samuel Richardson's correspondence, for example, William McCarthy has painstakingly analyzed the evidence of Richardson's surviving manuscript letters in comparison with those in the printed edition to test the frequent accusation that Barbauld flagrantly altered, abridged, and spliced together her subject's original manuscripts. This analysis has enabled McCarthy not only to determine which markings on the manuscripts are Barbauld's, as opposed to those of Richardson, various family editors, and even printshop workers, but also to carry out a statistical analysis of Barbauld's editorial actions and even to deduce the adversarial relations between Barbauld as painstaking editor and Richard Phillips as publisher insisting on speed above all. The result of McCarthy's comparative study is a radical rehabilitation of his subject as editor and a valuable insight into the methods of a turn-of-the-century publisher.[17] McCarthy's study of Barbauld's editing of Richardson's letters unexpectedly reveals as well the degree to which Richardson himself was the first mediator of his own manuscripts, altering and recopying them with imagined future print audiences in mind. Thus the example of the Barbauld edition highlights the changes to which even letter manuscripts, as textual objects existing in an intermedial ecosystem, are continually subject, whether they are reproduced in facsimile, print, or digital form. Richardson's letters, and the additional handwriting and other marks that appear on them, demonstrate that manuscripts often reflect interventions made at various times, by various people, and that with meticulous study (and the aid of contextualizing evidence), it can be possible to decipher the different hands, the stages of revision, and the purpose behind these marks (Figure 4). These manuscripts also reveal that the concepts of "draft" and "fair copy," terms that attempt to distinguish between incomplete and complete manuscript works, in fact exist on a continuum, as fair copies are transformed back into drafts through the processes of revision and correction.[18]

A manuscript page could be amended in many ways, and only some of these practices are recoverable. In one instance, a strike-through might allow us to read what was written beneath; in another, the original words might not be legible. A page could be removed entirely from a notebook, leaving no trace except possibly a stub of paper; another piece of paper could be sewn, pasted, or otherwise attached to conceal, sometimes permanently, what was originally beneath. From ink or handwriting we can sometimes discern the order in which changes were made,

---

[17] McCarthy deduces that Phillips' haste resulted in typesetting directly from original letters rather than the transcripts Barbauld had insisted on, as well as last-minute deletions of passages in the printing house ("Anna Barbauld," pp. 191–223).

[18] In the similar case of the novel *Frankenstein*, discussed in Section 4, there are differing degrees of revision to the pages within the draft notebooks, and even the fair copy manuscript is not perfectly fair.

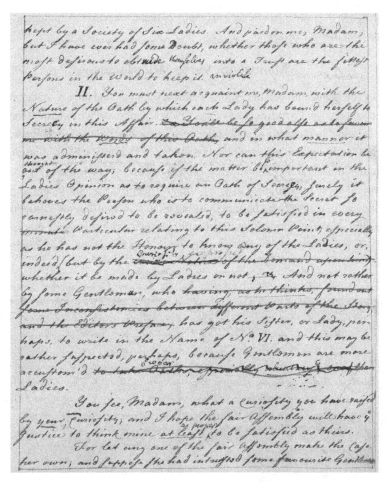

Figure 4 The second page of a retained letter, in a copyist's hand, from Samuel Richardson to "Six Reading Ladies," c. March 1742, Forster Collection XVI, 1, f.20, showing subsequent changes in Richardson's own shaky, elderly hand of the late 1750s and in Barbauld's paler ink. © Victoria and Albert Museum, London.

but we often cannot make these determinations. In these ways, manuscripts are incomplete witnesses to their history. At the other extreme, fair copy manuscripts with few markings, though they hide the writing process, can tell us a great deal about how literary texts circulated; the existence of variant fair copies of a single literary work, for example, can delineate a social circle and also point to ways literature was contextualized and personalized for different audiences over time. While the stories uncovered through manuscript study vary widely, the cases examined in this Element yield knowledge of literary sociability and production in the eighteenth century that could not be gained by any other means. These rewards, and the challenges we face in pursuit of them, are reflected throughout our discussions in this Element.

2 Manuscript Verse Miscellanies

During the eighteenth century, young women, old men, and anyone in between who could read and write and had access to texts, paper, and writing implements might at some point create a manuscript verse miscellany of their own. Extant in libraries, archives, and private collections today are hundreds, likely thousands, of such volumes, each to some degree a coherent aestheticized object (Figure 5).

Typical verse miscellanies offer a collection of predominantly contemporary, generally short poetry copied in a single hand, very often including local or "original" verse from within the compiler's own circle alongside materials taken from print sources such as magazines. In most cases, they begin as

Figure 5 A sampling of manuscript verse miscellany covers (Beinecke Osborn c.149; c.258; c.154; c.169) from the James Marshall and Marie-Louise Osborn Collection, Beinecke Rare Book and Manuscript Library, Yale University.

a bound book of blank paper; the poetry is copied in a careful, fair hand, often with uniform, decorative flourishes between items, sometimes with the addition of title pages, signatures, tables of contents, and even illustrations. These shared features suggest that their compilers were working with a sense of certain common practices for creating something new from available poetic materials. However, as Oliver Pickering has written of the manuscript miscellanies in the Brotherton Collection at the University of Leeds, each book represents "a unique act of compilation arising out of a particular set of circumstances" that makes it "more than the sum of its parts."[19] Why was this act of curation undertaken? Who was its creator, and who did they imagine as the audience for this book? What tastes or conventions guided the choice and arrangements of contents? Finally, what do these patterns make legible about poetic culture in the eighteenth century? Exploring such questions can reveal something about how individuals who were not cultural elites or metropolitan literary professionals encountered, engaged with, and created poetry.

In particular, such books reveal the inherent sociability of poetic culture, whereby the production, circulation, and reception of verse were woven into educated individuals' social networks. Manuscript poetry books attest to their function as objects of entertainment, education, and commemoration, in the form of occasional verse addressed to immediate family members and close friends; lines discussing local events; adaptations or imitations of popular poems to make them personal; and performative works of wit and formal complexity that are clearly intended to enhance a literary reputation. When their compilers and geographical origins can be determined, manuscript verse compilations provide valuable documentation of little-known literary networks of the time, whether school- and university-based coteries, interconnected Bluestocking circles, fashionable English and Irish coteries that overlapped at the cottage of the "Ladies of Llangollen,"[20] or the far-flung Quaker movement that created an identity for itself through poetry and letters. Together, manuscript verse miscellanies demonstrate the role of verse in everyday life, providing a context for the more well-documented sociable authorship of writers such as Jonathan Swift and Jane Austen. This section will discuss a compilation found by Betty Schellenberg, one of this Element's authors, in the Chawton House Library in Hampshire, England, illustrating how she pieced together at least some of the story of the book and the literary

---

[19] Pickering, "The BCMSV Database," p. 25.

[20] Lady Eleanor Butler and Sarah Ponsonby, whose forty-year "retirement" in North Wales attracted much admiration and poetry.

sociability embedded in its pages.[21] One theme of this compilation is the celebration of leading women, suggesting that scribal authorship might have sustained poetic traditions that did not welcome the more public glare of print. At another level, the miscellany reflects the affective, educational, and memorial functions of collecting poetry within the gentry and middle classes, and by extension, in the lives of individuals on the margins of public literary culture.

2.1 Engaging a Manuscript Poetry Miscellany

In the spring of 2017, when I was privileged to hold a fellowship at Chawton House, I was handed a package of manuscripts cataloged simply as "Wilmot, Elizabeth Sarah, Three manuscript notebooks of verse, 4946 WIL." Opening the first notebook, a small quarto covered with marbled paper (Figure 6), I found on the inside cover the signature "Elizabeth Sarah Wilmot 1771," followed by a list of contents in a more informal hand (Figure 7). This signature matched the hand

Figure 6 The cover of Elizabeth Sarah Wilmot's first notebook, 4946 WIL, Chawton House Library.

---

[21] To capture Schellenberg's experience of working with this manuscript, Section 2.1 adopts a first-person voice.

Figure 7 The inside front cover of Elizabeth Sarah Wilmot's first notebook, 4946 WIL, Chawton House Library.

and title of the remaining two notebooks, labeled "ES Wilmot's Verses 1773" and "ES Wilmot 1776" (later altered to "ES Wilmot's Verses"), respectively (Figure 8).

What ensued was a process typical of manuscript research when one encounters materials created by writers unknown to literary history. Often kept for a century or two by their creator's family or friends, such manuscripts may come to an archive along with family papers or some other contextualizing collection, but since they were initially created for audiences who knew what they were seeing, they often do not present themselves in ways that are readily intelligible. In this case, even the context was nonexistent: Chawton House has no record of the provenance of the notebooks, which the catalog describes

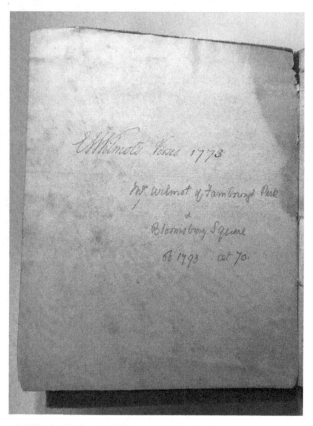

Figure 8 Elizabeth Sarah Wilmot's signature inside the front cover of the second notebook, 4946 WIL, Chawton House Library. The form of the "ESW" letters closely matches the "SW" signature at the bottom of two of the notebook 1 poems (Figure 10). The later annotation erroneously identifies "ESWilmot" as Mrs. Wilmot who died in 1793.

briefly as "verse on family matters written between 1744 and 1785 by Elizabeth Sarah Wilmot, of Farnborough Park, Hampshire." On the verso of the second leaf of the first notebook, I read, again in the more informal hand: "Verses written by my Dear Mama Sarah Wilmot at sundry times." A later annotation of this label told me that Mrs. Wilmot of Farnborough Park had died in 1793 at the age of sixty-nine; a similar annotation of "ES Wilmot" in the second notebook again identified the same Mrs. Wilmot. Based on the catalog entry and these signatures and annotations, I began with the assumption that the poet and compiler of the three books was a Mrs. Elizabeth Sarah Wilmot who had been known as Sarah, and whose first book had later been annotated by a daughter or son. In fact, almost every poem in the book was signed by a distinctive scrawl-like device that can be read as an "S" or "Se," supporting the theory that Elizabeth Sarah had gone by the name Sarah or even used an inverted version of her two given names (Figure 9).

Online searches yielded transcriptions of memorials in St. Peter's Church of Farnborough, Hampshire, including Henry Wilmot, d. 1794, aged eighty-four, and his wife Sarah Wilmot, d. 1793 at the age of sixty-nine. The dates were right, but nowhere was this Sarah Wilmot referred to as Elizabeth Sarah or Sarah Elizabeth. When the monuments at St. Peter's yielded a further memorial for "Elizabeth Sarah Wife of James Seton of London and Daughter of Henry and Sarah Wilmot," who died on February 5, 1803, aged forty-three, the clues

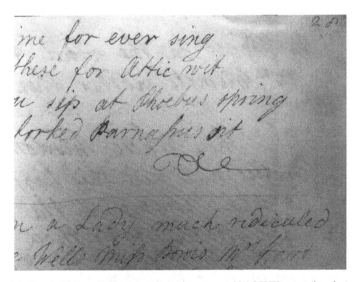

Figure 9 Sarah Wilmot's "S" or "Se" signature, 4946 WIL, notebook 1, p. 28 detail, Chawton House Library; this mark is found at the end of most of the poems in the first notebook.

realigned themselves: Elizabeth Sarah was Sarah Wilmot's daughter, born between February 1759 and January 1760, who would have been just eleven or twelve years old in 1771 when she signed and dated the first notebook – too young to be composing such poetry, but old enough to begin to copy out her mother's poems. This hypothesis was supported by the headers of the poems, which indicate a third-person perspective and a need to spell out the occasion of writing for the notebook's potential readers – for example, "Epitaph / On Mrs Mary Lamb Novr: 1767 who had lived twelve years with Mrs Wilmot first as her own maid & afterward as housekeeper & married in her service."

Returning to the puzzle of the signature, I observed that in addition to the "S" or "Se" mark, a more calligraphic device is found in notebook one. This more elaborate form appears to be an "SW," clearly produced by the same hand as that of the "ESWilmot's Verses 1773" of the second notebook, shown in Figure 8. The elaborate "SW" occurs twice, once alone and once, after the penultimate poem, above the simpler "S" (Figure 10).

I now believe that Sarah checked and endorsed with her scrawl device the copies made by Elizabeth Sarah, who in two cases marked her completed copy with her mother's initials. It appears, then, that notebook one is in the hand of Sarah Wilmot's daughter, Elizabeth Sarah. The booklet may well be the product of a pedagogical exercise when eleven-year-old Elizabeth Sarah was being educated at home in handwriting, poetry, and taste but had not yet begun to

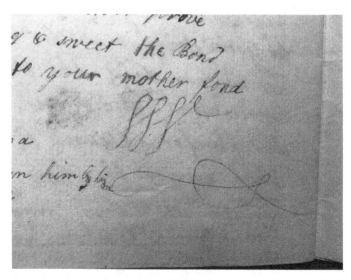

Figure 10 Elizabeth Sarah's notation "SW" at the bottom of her mother's poem to her son Valentine Henry, followed by Sarah's endorsement. Notebook 1, p. 49 detail, 4946 WIL, Chawton House Library.

write poetry of her own. As Kathleen Keown has argued, the production of occasional poetry was often among the polite accomplishments considered important for genteel young women of the period; it would not be surprising that her mother, herself a practiced poet, took care to instruct her daughter in the art.[22] This interpretation is reinforced by the fact that the important final position in the notebook is given to a poem praising Elizabeth Sarah's budding efforts to pursue the Muses. It begins: "My Dearest Child my much loved Treasure/ Your lines I read with rap'trous pleasure/ To see the sacred Sisters thus inspire/ Your early Mind with their poetic fire." As one of my students wrote of it, "the lavish praise Wilmot gives her daughter serves as encouragement to join" the "tradition of sharing and supporting writing" that was a feature of the Bluestocking networks.[23]

I have outlined the extended process of piecing together this book's story to illustrate the false starts and imaginative engagements involved in such work. The motivation to pursue the chase, however, was what I found as I immersed myself in the contents of this first notebook. From previous work with manuscript verse miscellanies, I assumed I would be reading a sprinkling of occasional poems by an obscure provincial lady, interspersed among verse copied from contemporary print sources or contributed by members of her circle. Indeed, in this first notebook there were the verses marking family events: "To Mr Morris on his wedding-day," "To Mrs Morris on her birth-day by her Daughter Mrs Wilmot January 7th 1746/7," "From Mrs Wilmot in the Country to Mr Wilmot in Town Decr: 11th 1754," and so on. While there did not seem to be any poems copied from print, there was a short, witty piece by the retired celebrity actor and theater manager David Garrick urging his physician friend William Cadogan to stop displaying his lack of taste by criticizing Shakespeare. From the start, however, I was struck by how unusually accomplished Mrs. Wilmot's poetry was. The fourth poem, for example, "A Monody to the Memory of Mrs. Cadogan upon reading Milton's Lycidas by her particular friend Mrs Wilmot" – opens with a strikingly rhythmic and polished invocation of the muse:

> Once more my broken Lyre I'll string,
> Once more will taste the hallow'd spring,
> And visit Phoebus' shrine.
> Again I'll tempt the with'ring bay,
> And to entune this mournfull lay
> Implore the sacred Nine.

[22] Keown, "Eighteenth-Century Women's Poetry."

[23] Paul, "Comparing," n.p. This analysis is part of "Sarah Wilmot, Forgotten Bluestocking," a collaborative student edition of seven of Wilmot's previously unpublished poems: https://sarahwilmot.omeka.net/

It made sense that the notebook would be almost entirely devoted to her work, unlike many others where original poetry is minimal or nonexistent; Mrs. Wilmot must have had somewhat of a reputation as a social author.

The first real shock of recognition, however, occurred in the ninth poem, a mock-epic account of a chess match addressed "To Mrs Howe" and, on the basis of internal evidence, composed in about 1760. When this poem posed a rhetorical question:

> Have I not seen thee then triumphant sit
> Bearing from Carter Montagu and Pitt
> The palm of Science judgement attic lore
> While blushing they submitted to thy pow'r[?]

I could not miss the reference to a short-lived configuration of leading Bluestocking women – Elizabeth Carter, Elizabeth Montagu, and Anne Pitt. This inherently unstable grouping, as Deborah Heller has anatomized it, existed only between 1759 and 1761, after which Montagu turned definitively from Pitt's brilliantly unstable wit toward the more intellectually and morally serious Carter. Wilmot is thus recording her proximity to the Bluestocking phenomenon right at the point of its emergence.[24] Poem twelve in the collection, titled "The Mistake Rectified April 1770" (Figure 11), underscored the significance of Carter and Montagu for Wilmot. In a series of seventeen carefully numbered stanzas, Apollo and the Muses, "sauntring" about on Mount Parnassus, try to identify a mysterious woman drinking from the Castalian spring. Fourteen leading contemporary women are proposed as candidates and praised in turn, before the poem deduces, with the help of Shakespeare, that the "learned fair" is "Montagu," to whom Shakespeare is grateful for the "gen'rous love/ [That] Has from the critic saved my Fame." The very specific dating of this poem – April 1770 – now came into focus for me: Elizabeth Montagu had published her famous *Essay on the Writings and Genius of Shakespear ... with Some Remarks upon the Misrepresentations of Mons. de Voltaire* in May 1769, and the work's authorship had gradually become known through the final months of the same year; its second edition appeared in 1770. I was reading what is known as a "Sessions of the Poets" poem, a witty subgenre in which Apollo is called upon to adjudicate the claims of a competing group of contemporary writers. As this section will go on to explain, the tradition tended to be masculine and misogynistic; its use for a poem honoring Montagu and also, it seemed, a whole collection of admirable women, hinted at a possible manuscript-based

---

[24] Heller, "Bluestockings and Virtue Friendship."

The Mistake Rectified April 1770

1

Apollo sauntring with the Nine
About his fam'd Parnassian mount
Observed a Female near his shrine
Who freely quaffed the sacred fount

2

Fair Clio said 'tis Spencer's air
I know her mild majestic Style
Thalia cryd I must declare
'Tis Egremonts attractive smile

3

Sure Denbighs heart is in those eyes
So full of sweetness Friendship Love
It must be her Calliop cry's
But let's approach & nearer prove

4

A calm that goodness bosoms ever
Made grave Melpomene incline
To name Boscawen for she never
Could be unthought of by the Nine

5

One sprightly Walsingham could see
Whose lively wit is sure to please
Another said that could not be
For that she knew Howes well bred ease

6 .

Both then retracting could descry
Learn'd Temples quick Pathetic look
Then Dunbars grace so winning shy
All said could never be mistook

7

Loved Penn and Shelburne each were guess'd
An anxious soft Maternal air
So well their gentle Minds expressed
'Twas one of them or Finch was clear

8

Urania look'd & cryed you're right
Tho' in the name you are mistaken
'Tis Pomfrets blood I'm sure at sight
But I am certain it is Clayton.

9

Polymnia then Erato moved
(By her own Lute lulled half asleep)

'Tis Coningesby they instant proved
For who besides dared drink so deep

10

When Phoebus smiling bowed around
I hope fair Nymphs you'll own my claim
A Fathers feeling speak aloud
It must be her my favourite name

11

'Tis Carter readily I trace
Her placid smile & brow serene
Her timid meek and even pace
Her unaffected easy mein

12

Then Shakespear who unseen had been
Reposing on a bed of Roses
Listening to all this comic Scene
The Mystery at last discloses

13

Aonian Maids 'tis very strange
That ye whose downy feathered feet
Trip dayly o'er this velvet range
And know each Votarys retreat

14

And you bright Phoebus stranger still
Whom all the Deities declare
The Master of this forked Hill
Should so mistake this learned Fair

15

Who erst in beautys bud was led
Full oft to sip your hallow'd spring
The Syren voice of flatt'ry fled
Herself your praises here to sing

16

Nor has her ripen'd mind e'er burn'd
For titles wealth ambition vain
But from them all has frequent turn'd
To join your Scientific train

17

Let me however gratefull prove
And pay my Tribute just her claim
To Montagu whose gen'rous love
Has from the critic saved my Fame

Figure 11 Transcription of "The Mistake Rectified" by Sarah Wilmot,
notebook 1, pp. 42–46, 4946 WIL, Chawton House Library.

resistance to this tradition. To borrow Pickering's phrasing, the "particular set of circumstances" out of which Mrs. Wilmot's poetry arose, what made this notebook "more than the sum of its parts," was its apparent insider perspective on an important eighteenth-century cultural phenomenon, its hints of a hitherto-hidden network of literary exchange between country gentlewomen, and its demonstration of how a daughter might be educated in the mid-eighteenth century.

I was now keen to find out more about the talented but unknown Mrs. Wilmot, and especially about her social and literary connections. Various genealogical sources, *Wikipedia*, eighteenth-century travel accounts, and the *Orlando* text-base entries for Wilmot's daughter-in-law all contributed insights. Sarah Morris Wilmot, born in 1723, was a close contemporary of the "Queen of the Blues" Elizabeth Robinson Montagu, born in 1718, and her younger sister Sarah Robinson Scott, born in 1720. The daughter of Colonel Valentine Morris and Elizabeth Wilmot Morris, she married her father's cousin Henry Wilmot, a barrister and from 1768 lord of the manor of Farnborough Park, Hampshire. Sarah's father was a West Indian planter and Sarah may have spent the early years of her life on a sugar plantation, but this origin is not mentioned in her verse. With his acquired wealth, Colonel Morris purchased the estate Piercefield in Wales, near Chepstow, and it is of Piercefield that she writes nostalgically in her extant poetry.[25] As for Elizabeth Sarah, she became a recognized pastel artist and the mother of a judge of the supreme court of Calcutta.

It is more difficult to tease out the formation of a manuscript poet's literary networks and her standing within them, even with the help of poems referencing her connections to well-known figures such as Montagu and Garrick. The Wilmots do feature in editions of Garrick's correspondence, although without any annotation of who they were. This friendship may have arisen with a connection between Henry Wilmot and Garrick. A collection of miscellaneous Garrick-related notes and poems at the Folger Shakespeare Library includes a short occasional poem on the 1766 appointment of Charles Pratt, Lord Camden, as lord chancellor; in these verses, Henry Wilmot serves as interlocutor and addressee of Garrick. A facetious 1771 note from Wilmot to Garrick claims that a Mr. Phillips is dunning him for a literal or metaphorical debt incurred by Garrick.[26] Subsequent correspondence makes it clear that Mrs. Wilmot herself was a conduit of news between the Garricks and their

---

[25] Sarah's brother Valentine inherited Piercefield in 1743 and developed it into a much-admired stop on the domestic tour, but he bankrupted himself through this and other ventures; the estate was sold in 1784.

[26] Folger Shakespeare Library MS Y.1089, No. 10, titled "Wilmot and Garrick Upon Lord Camden's taking the Great Seal"; Garrick, *Private Correspondence*, vol. 1, p. 428.

friends, as well as an influence broker, bringing authors to Garrick's attention and working with him to assist others through her connections with aristocrats. The playwright Elizabeth Griffith, for example, writes to Garrick in 1770 that "Our good and amiable Mrs. Wilmot told me that you were involved in so many engagements to authors, that you regretted it was not in your power to receive any piece from me." On another occasion, Garrick tells Sarah, "Your friendship and affection is all turnpike [i.e., a smooth, modern roadway], and there is not a single jog upon the whole road."[27] The embeddedness of Garrick's above-mentioned playful attack on Dr. Cadogan in a network of literary sociability that included Garrick, the Wilmots, and the Cadogan family is evidenced by the conclusion of a 1773 letter to Garrick from Dr. John Hoadly: "In return for this [some enclosed lines of verse], I expect you to send me the wit between Dr. Cadogan and you, which made his daughter cry at Mr. Wilmot's."[28] In this world, literary production is an everyday sociable pleasure, and wit and influence are wielded in tandem, leaving their traces in the manuscript forms of correspondence and the poetry miscellany.

2.2 "The Mistake Rectified"

Sarah Wilmot's place in Elizabeth Montagu's Bluestocking network is more difficult to trace, in part because the vast Montagu correspondence has never been published in its entirety. Montagu and her sister Sarah Scott do casually mention the exchange of books and letters to and from Mrs. Wilmot in their letters to each other, and in 1769, the Wilmots dined at least once with Montagu while accompanying their son back to Eton.[29] An anonymous manuscript poem in the Montagu Collection whose author had not previously been identified, the monody on the death of Frances Cadogan quoted earlier, can now be attributed to Wilmot on the evidence of the Chawton House notebooks. Although there was significant overlap between the Bluestocking and Garrick social circles,[30] there may have been an older, familial connection between Montagu and Wilmot. "Morris," Wilmot's maiden name, was also the maiden name of Montagu's maternal grandmother; the family home of "Mount Morris" in Kent was Elizabeth's mother's inheritance; the name was not only adopted by the eldest Robinson brother upon his inheritance of Mount Morris but was also the given name of another of Elizabeth's brothers. Thus "The Mistake

---

[27] *Correspondence of Garrick*, vol. 1, p. 386; vol. 2, p. 358; see also vol. 2, p. 357 regarding Garrick and Sarah Wilmot's efforts to arrange for a clerical living for an acquaintance.

[28] *Correspondence of Garrick*, vol. 1, p. 526.

[29] Elizabeth Montagu to Sarah Scott, 11 & 12 Dec. 1764, the Huntington Library, mo5814; Elizabeth Montagu to Edward Montagu, 10 & 11 September 1769, Huntington mo2719.

[30] The Montagu Collection also contains Garrick's lines on Cadogan.

Rectified" was surely composed to be shared with Montagu and likely Carter and other women it describes, just as an earlier manuscript poem "The Circuit of Appollo [*sic*]," written at the turn of the century by the celebrated poet Anne Finch, Lady Winchilsea (1661–1720), was composed to be circulated among a group of Kentish women poets Finch wanted to celebrate.

The lineage of the "Sessions of the Poets" subgenre has been traced through the seventeenth century by Claudia Thomas Kairoff.[31] Kairoff argues that Finch's "Circuit of Appollo" breaks with the casual misogyny of this tradition to praise a circle of local female poets in an equally witty but more mutually affirmative manner. The *mise-en-scène* of Finch's poem ends with Apollo declining to award the laurel wreath to any one poet, deciding at the last moment that it is not advisable to arouse female jealousy by selecting one woman over the others. On the way, however, Finch has referenced six female poets, mentioning Katherine Phillips and assessing Aphra Behn, before praising the achievements of four contemporaries.[32] Wilmot's poem shares with Finch's not only a focus on an interconnected network of accomplished women but also an affirmative spirit: she finds something to praise in each of a succession of women before awarding the ultimate prize to Montagu. Although the form and meter of the two poems differ, Wilmot echoes Finch in the conversational humor of the scene, and in the prominent role assigned to the Muses. In Finch's poem, the Nine are left to decide the question when Apollo absconds; in Wilmot's, they conduct the initial review of women until Apollo and Shakespeare step forward to determine the identity of the mysterious female who is "freely quaff[ing]" Apollo's "sacred fount."

At the same time, there are significant differences between the two poems. These differences can be seen as reflective of a more public cultural role for the women named by Wilmot, one mediated through print-based celebrity. Even though, like Finch, she is apparently writing a poem for coterie circulation, Wilmot names fifteen women in all, and she does so explicitly, rather than using the typical pastoral pseudonyms that create an effect of "intentional obscurity" in the earlier poem.[33] In fact, nine of Wilmot's fifteen subjects are identified not by Christian name but by aristocratic title, signaling their status and position through marriage in a patrilineal social hierarchy. Lady Juliana Penn; her sister Charlotte Finch; and their niece Sophia Carteret, wife of the second Earl of

---

[31] Kairoff, "Tracing 'The Circuit of Appollo,'" pp. 21–35.

[32] These contemporaries have been identified as Elizabeth Taylor Withens, Grace Blome Randolph, Sarah Dixon, and Finch herself. Kairoff notes that Randolph in turn supplied one of the poems of commendation that introduce Finch's folio manuscript of poems, in which Randolph references the earlier "Circuit" poem (p. 29). Thus it can be surmised that Finch's poem was circulated at least to the three women praised in this playful contest.

[33] Kairoff, p. 26.

Shelburne, are explicitly grouped together by "blood," as the daughters and granddaughter, respectively, of the first Earl of Pomfret. Thus, the overall effect of naming in the first half of the poem is one of public, stylized display – a red-carpet parade, or perhaps a formal court presentation – rather than intimate mutual praise and encouragement. The poem reflects Clarissa Campbell Orr's observation that in the first decades of King George III's reign, court culture and Bluestocking culture were very much aligned, precisely through individuals such as Lady Charlotte Finch and Lord and Lady Shelburne, and around cultural projects such as the promotion of the arts and sciences and the moral education of the nation's leaders.[34]

Given the prominence of naming and pedigree in this poem, it is perhaps not surprising that "The Mistake Rectified" limits its praise of most of its subjects to a single attribute or two, and that those attributes tend not to literary production or even conversational skills but rather outwardly visible traits – a "mild majestic Style," an "attractive smile," "a calm that goodness bosoms ever," or "an anxious soft Maternal air." Even Elizabeth Carter, the penultimate female figure and "favourite" of Phoebus whom the reader would recognize as a poet and translator of the Greek Stoic philosopher Epictetus, is commended for "Her placid smile & brow serene/ Her timid meek and even pace/ Her unaffected easy mein [*sic*]." In short, one might on first reading conclude that admirable female publicity among the Bluestocking network, or at least in Mrs. Wilmot's view, must adhere to traditional social hierarchies and to rigid expectations of modesty, grace, and maternal softness.

Like Finch's "Circuit of Appollo," the poem can nevertheless be appreciated as a celebration of female intellectual achievement, one that is of its particular time and context. First, the conceit of the poem rests on the implicit claim that these women need no introduction, that Apollo and the Muses should be able to recognize from a single external sign exactly who these women are and what they stand for. The approach is at once distant and familiar: since everyone knows what each of the women is famous for, it hardly needs to be said. In this respect, Wilmot's poem becomes a kind of harbinger of the decade of the 1770s, when the iconography of female achievement became a frequent feature of patriotic public culture. Second, a number of the descriptions convey more than what first appears to the twenty-first-century reader. The ancestral gesture to Pomfret blood described earlier was likely heard by Wilmot's first audience as matrilineal rather than patrilineal, a reference to the three women's mother and grandmother Henrietta Fermor, Countess of Pomfret, known for her literary correspondences with an earlier generation of learned women. Those seemingly

---

[34] Orr, "Queen of the Blues," pp. 233–53.

superficial and clichéd descriptions are in fact revealing. For example, the Muses' debate about whether it is Penn, Shelburne, or Finch who displays "an anxious soft Maternal air" may be less about idealizing women's natural maternal qualities than about a more specialized expertise: Lady Juliana Penn was very involved in the management of her husband's three-quarter share of the Pennsylvania colony on behalf of her family; Lady Shelburne was known for the care that she and her husband, the second Earl, were devoting to the education of their sons; and Lady Charlotte Finch was governess to the royal children.[35] Even the description of Carter as above all "placid," "serene," and moving at an "easy" pace evokes the Stoic philosophy that she had helped popularize.

A final indication that this poem values female intellectual achievement is found in its overall trajectory toward the culminating description of Montagu. Arguably the poem moves in a deliberate progression through its list of aristocrats toward an increasing emphasis on education and learning. Montagu is specifically praised as a "learned Fair," one who "fled" "flatt'ry" even in her time of youthful beauty to sing the praises of Apollo, one who possesses a "ripen'd mind," and who turns away from "titles wealth ambition" to join the "Scientific train." As the culminating character sketch of the poem and the description of the contest winner, Montagu's portrait represents an ideal use of female wit. A non-aristocrat, Montagu here is made notable not for her beauty, wealth, or social connections, all of which were indeed conspicuous, but rather for her learning and contribution to literary criticism. Her emergence as the contest winner can be read as underscoring the poem's implied critique of another kind of conspicuous woman: overtly political aristocrats like the Duchesses of Bedford, Northumberland, or Devonshire who wielded formidable dynastic political power through elections and patronage.[36] Mrs. Wilmot, it seems, believed that women had a public cultural role to play, and she was prepared to name the women she admired for doing so.

2.3 A Female Literary Tradition in Manuscript?

Of the fifteen Sarah Wilmot poems preserved in the first notebook, five of them can be seen as explicitly celebrating or defending women's talents and achievements. Besides two poems honoring Frances Cadogan, the account of an epic chess match between two women, and "The Mistake Rectified," another notable poem in the book, "To Dr Bartholomew at Tunbridge Wells on his having wrote many Lampoons Satyrs &c," admonishes the addressee in 1759 to turn away from satires of women in favor of an array of fourteen admirable women, from

---

[35] Orr, pp. 244–45.　　[36] These politically active women are discussed in Chalus, *Elite Women*.

the Duchess of Richmond to Wilmot's own sister Caroline Morris. Singing their praises, the speaker promises, would allow Bartholomew to exercise his "Attic wit" and "sip at Phebus' spring/ And on the forked Parnassus sit."[37] Given her commitment to acknowledging female worthies in her poetry, the question arises as to whether Wilmot might have known of the "Circuit of Appollo" poem composed by her Kentish predecessor. While we have so far no evidence for Finch's "Sessions" verses having appeared anywhere in print between her death in 1720 and the 1759–70 dates of these poems, there are a number of linked networks through which limited manuscript circulation might have occurred. Although space constraints prohibit full elaboration here, one possible route is copies of Finch's poems in the possession of Finch's great-niece Frances Thynne Seymour, the Countess of Hertford (later Duchess of Somerset); we know that Hertford showed her collections of manuscripts to guests such as Catherine Talbot, friend of Carter and Montagu, and Thomas Birch, both featured in Section 3. An additional probability, suggested earlier, is that the living female poets described in Finch's "Circuit of Appollo" would have received copies from her, which might have resulted in a fairly robust, if controlled, circulation of the verses. Such a poem might have been particularly valued within networks of country gentlewomen who would have enjoyed its sly celebration of the renown of provincial poets like themselves. All of this might have been true without the poem ever escaping the confines of a few select provincial networks.

Elizabeth Montagu's publication of *An Essay on the Writings and Genius of Shakespear* in 1769 might be seen as a point of arrival in the unofficial campaign of Bluestocking women to influence the social, moral, and cultural realms. Such influence operated not only through the conversational gatherings they hosted in their drawing rooms during the London season but also through their actions as overseers of families and estates from their residences in the country – spheres of action linked by correspondence networks whereby poems of commendation circulated as well. Within such channels of controlled circulation, influential poems may have generated other works without our being aware of the chain of transmission. If we cannot as yet trace the place of "The Mistake Rectified" in a manuscript literary tradition, an awareness of how the world of literary sociability functioned indicates that such a tradition may, indeed, stretch all the way back to Anne Finch's "Circuit of Appollo."[38]

Paula Backscheider has pointed out that the sheer quantity of women's poetry that has likely been lost makes it nearly impossible to determine whether the

---

[37] Wilmot, Notebook 1, f. 28.
[38] Backscheider, *Eighteenth-Century Women Poets,* pp. 386–87.

poetry we do have is part of a larger pattern or tradition. Discovering Sarah Wilmot's previously unknown poems enables us to trace new lines of connection between literary women and men of the Bluestocking era. Beyond this level of historical evidence, what is the value of such findings for the researcher of eighteenth-century literary culture? First, the notebooks Elizabeth Sarah created as a girl illustrate the place of poetry in educational practice, particularly for women. Over the course of the three books, we see a young adolescent learning, by copying her mother's most important poems, not only fluid handwriting but also elegant poetic expression and the social function of verse and wit in the maintenance of social ties. Second, Wilmot's use of several of her major poems to celebrate female friendship, intelligence, and achievement in the arts and education can be seen as preserving a mid-century spirit of female solidarity and initiative, and as passing that legacy on to her daughter. Finally, the poems' allusive and imitative character also hints at a counter-canon of writings that coterie authors might have appreciated and been influenced by, even as some of these works may now have been lost to our knowledge. Such canons may include, as in this case, feminocentric works such as Pope's representation of Belinda's mock-epic triumph at ombre[39] but also Finch's "Circuit of Appollo."

Manuscript records can help fill gaps that we did not even know existed. If they can bring to light the poems of a networker like Sarah Wilmot who for unknown reasons chose to remain "hidden" in coterie circles, they may also do so for lost works of writers like Phillis Wheatley, profoundly marginalized by intersecting conditions of status, religious affiliation, geographical location, and race. Often the record of those who are obscure or marginalized in their own times, through choice or obstruction, becomes fragmentary or even disappears from literary history. By contrast, our next section looks at how much carefully preserved collections of the correspondence of culturally prominent individuals can reveal about literary sociability in the eighteenth century.

3 Familiar Correspondences

This section will consider the familiar correspondence, both as a guide to how literary sociability functioned in the eighteenth century and as a creative artifact in its own right. As described in Section 1, the familiar letter is a handwritten text that at once documents and bears the physical traces of the labor of letter writing, as it was variously facilitated, structured, or impeded by geographical location, postal schedules, social networks, medical conditions, and even the seasons of the year. The familiar letter was also, in the eighteenth century,

---

[39]　Wilmot's poem "To Mrs Howe on her challenging Mrs Morris to a game of Chess" recounts a chess match reminiscent of the game of ombre in Canto 3 of Pope's *Rape of the Lock.*

a valued literary form. Eighteenth-century writers and readers were attuned to epistolarity as a skill to be nurtured, wielded for strategic purposes, and appreciated for the instruction and entertainment it offered. For scholars today, extended familiar correspondences, in particular those that follow a social relationship and the dialogue it generates over a period of many years, offer us not simply a record of friendships, composition processes, or publishing transactions but also a picture of how sociable literary networks might be built over time, how tastes and critical principles might be developed through dialogue, and how letters were received and circulated as literary objects. In this section, three long-term correspondences (lasting between twenty-five and seventy years) will be used to illustrate each of these dimensions in turn. As an ensemble, the three demonstrate how a correspondence can be approached as a collaborative text that develops and documents its own unique terms and identities.

Our three examples are drawn from a 1741–65 series of weekly letters between Philip Yorke, son of Lord Chancellor Hardwick, and the editor-historian Thomas Birch; the exchanges spanning an even longer period, from the late 1730s to 1770, between Yorke's wife Jemima, the Marchioness Grey, and her childhood friend Catherine Talbot; and the extensive corresponding networks of Elizabeth Montagu, the Bluestocking hostess introduced in Section 2, with family members, female and male Bluestocking friends, literary figures, and business contacts, extending through almost seven decades up to 1799. Despite their shared longevity, these correspondences differ in the social dynamics between their participants, the functions performed by the ensemble of exchanges, and their literary historical significance. They also vary in their preservation histories, from their first creation to the present. It is with questions of preservation that this section begins.

3.1 The Materiality of Correspondences

In any study of a correspondence, it is necessary to distinguish between its ideal form – that is, the complete set of exchanges between two or more individuals, which generally exists only in theory – and the actual materials that have survived. Surviving documents may be drafts or retained copies; sent letters might have miscarried before reaching their intended recipient. Letters safely delivered might subsequently be damaged, lost, or destroyed. While correspondences were rarely published as printed books in their authors' lifetimes,[40]

---

[40] One such publication is Astell and Norris, *Letters Concerning the Love of God*, first published in 1705. Bigold, *Women of Letters*, has examined the mixed fates of literary women originally known for their letter writing in scribal circles as those letters moved into print, whether during their lifetimes or posthumously.

many were preserved by their writers and/or recipients in manuscript form, often bundled, sewn, or bound together according to correspondent. Such collecting practices indicate the value placed upon the familiar letter, especially as part of an extended epistolary exchange. These practices also were the first determiners of what is available to us today, and in what form. Any study of correspondence, like other manuscript studies, must therefore consider the peculiar vicissitudes to which a series of discrete documents produced over many years and in various locations may be subject.

Since temporal gaps are inherent in correspondence as a medium, its twenty-first -century reader must interpret whether such gaps in the record mean nothing at all, simply registering through silence a period when the correspondents were within reach of regular conversation, or whether they signal a rupture in the social bond or the destruction or loss of materials sometime in the afterlife of the exchange. As an example of the former, the Yorke-Birch letters are carefully bound into folio volumes as a complete set, yet they exhibit annual gaps when both men were resident in London. With the Montagu correspondence, on the other hand, letters from the sensitive 1751–52 period in which Elizabeth's sister Sarah was forcibly separated by her family from her husband George Lewis Scott have disappeared, likely deliberately destroyed in an attempt to preserve family secrets. Most of Talbot's letters to Grey are believed to have been accidentally discarded in the process of sorting Grey's papers after her death.[41] Thus, a correspondence in manuscript may survive in any number of states, from a one-sided fragment to a set of bound volumes entirely recopied in the uniform hand of a descendant.

In the Montagu case, many of the original manuscripts were preserved, embellished with her nephew and heir Matthew Montagu's editorial markings (and later, those of other editors). This allows for a comparison of the manuscript record with the four-volume selection published by Matthew between 1810 and 1813, revealing perspectives and methodologies very different from those of today's scholarly editor. The print edition of the letters, for example, almost entirely omits the greetings and miscellaneous items typically conveyed in the final paragraphs and postscripts of a letter – precisely those details from which a researcher might reconstruct patterns of book borrowing, for example, or the vectors of a network. This was common editorial practice for the period, but Matthew Montagu also expunges much of Elizabeth's sharp-tongued, colloquial commentary as well as details that highlight her dependent status as a companion to the Duchess of Portland – for example, her view of the clergyman Edward Young's satire of women ("for those Animals he has ridiculed it is not a farthing matter for them") disappears, while her being "invited

---
[41] Myers, *Bluestocking Circle*, p. 67.

along to Lady North's" to see the formal court dress of an assembled group of courtiers, becomes simply "I was at Lady North's."[42] Such alterations underscore the principle that best scholarly practice requires consultation of the physical manuscripts that comprise a correspondence, as opposed to later printings, when those exist.

Even when manuscripts survive, methods of preserving and cataloging can vary significantly, raising barriers to navigation and interpretation. Correspondent and/or date are the most common organizational systems but in vast assemblages such as the 6,923-piece Montagu Collection at the Huntington Library in San Marino California, even such logics leave difficulties. In that collection, the combination of numbering the individual letters in different sequences for each correspondent but then storing the entire collection in a chronologically ordered series of boxes, with no master inventory cross-referencing this information or documenting contents, for many years resulted in an archive searchable only by trial and error as to exactly how the letters of a particular correspondence might be distributed across the 117 boxes of the collection. (A 2015 finding aid available through the Online Archive of California has at last mitigated this.)[43] In a comparable case, that of the Forster Collection of Samuel Richardson's correspondence held in the Victoria and Albert Museum in London, six massive folio volumes created in the late nineteenth century are generally organized around discussion of the three Richardson novels, preserving the author's own mode of compilation.[44] The result is a collection that is not only extremely unwieldy, with quarto-sized letter paper glued at ninety-degree angles into two openings per page, but very challenging to search by correspondent or date in the absence of individual item labels (Figure 12).

As these two instances demonstrate, and as Section 5 will explore in greater detail, to study a correspondence in manuscript is to work through layers of physical and interpretive mediation even when a large proportion of its surviving components have been kept together. Almost always, some documents have found their way into archives on different continents: approximately one-quarter of the Montagu letters, for example, are held in locations other than the Huntington, and more are being found on a regular basis.

---

[42] Montagu to Scott, 8 and 14 Oct. 1740 (Montagu Collection mo5557 and mo5558) and 5 Feb. 1740/41 (mo5603), compared with Matthew Montagu, ed., *Letters of Mrs. Elizabeth Montagu*, 2.58–59 and 1.127. Future references to the Montagu Collection will reference the manuscript call number only.

[43] Ellis provides an overview of the Montagu Collection's preservation history in "Letters, Organization, and the Archive." For the finding aid, see https://oac.cdlib.org/findaid/ark:/13030/tf767nb23s/?query=Montagu+Collection.

[44] Keymer and Sabor, "General Editors' Preface," vol 1, pp. xi–xii.

Figure 12 [Arabella Churchill] to [Jane Collier], 30 June 1749, FM XV, 2, f. 22 in the Forster collection at the National Art Library, Victoria and Albert Museum, illustrating the insertion of letters at a ninety-degree angle to the page opening. © Victoria and Albert Museum, London.

Current digitization projects address some of these issues by reuniting letters in a virtual space, preserving fragile documents and offering searchable access to researchers for whom archival examination is not possible. As unique collections are digitized, it also becomes feasible to take a more holistic approach to them as extended, collaborative texts. The Montagu correspondence is currently being digitized and edited as the *Elizabeth Montagu Correspondence Online*, an open-access undertaking by a large, international team of scholars, supported by a substantial charitable trust as well as numerous institutions and research organizations;[45] this edition will enable the kind of comprehensive tracking of persons and subjects through the correspondence that has never before been possible. At the same time, digital remediations, like print editions, can flatten the complexity of letters as three-dimensional objects that bear witness to their history of folding, sealing, posting, docketing, bundling, and editing. The question of digital remediation is taken up in greater detail in Section 5 of this Element; this section will focus rather on what makes these

---

[45] *Elizabeth Montagu Correspondence Online*, http://emco.swansea.ac.uk/home/.

variously imperfect collections worthy of study, that is, on the insights they can yield into eighteenth-century lives lived in the Republic of Letters. In their individuality, even imperfectly preserved correspondences allow us to trace social authorship at work as familiar letters are composed and exchanged.

3.2 "Laudable Ardor": Philip Yorke and Thomas Birch

Held in the British Library as part of the Hardwicke Collection, the twenty-five-year weekly correspondence between Philip Yorke (1720–90), heir to the powerful Lord Chancellor Hardwicke, and Thomas Birch (1705–66), urban, middle-class clergyman, editor, and author, is preserved in a complete chronological sequence, carefully bound into five folio volumes. Although Birch, like Yorke, bequeathed to the British Museum (now the British Library) his voluminous historical papers and correspondence, the materials were not organized systematically as complete two-sided exchanges by Birch himself before his unexpected death. This sequence of weekly letters is an exception in its continuity and completeness, including Yorke's own contributions, which were likely returned to him by Birch's literary executor when the latter's death ended the exchange (Figure 13). This completeness is not simply the product of posthumous chance: the correspondence was viewed from the start as a work of periodical literary history, one that would both inform and entertain. It was therefore treated by both men in keeping with their shared historical aims. For today's reader, the cumulative sequence offers not only such a text but also the history of a personal relationship that cuts across traditional social boundaries to resemble a modern friendship.[46]

The Yorke-Birch correspondence demonstrates how a hierarchically organized social relationship could be transformed into a more egalitarian one through shared literary-historical endeavors in the Republic of Letters, as well as how the familiar letter itself was practiced and appreciated as a literary form. When Yorke married Jemima Campbell (1722–97), granddaughter and heiress to the Duke of Kent, in 1740, he left Cambridge and soon was based largely at the country estate of Wrest in Bedfordshire. In collaboration with a coterie consisting of his brother Charles; Cambridge friends and tutors; and Catherine Talbot, his wife's lifelong friend, he pursued his literary-historical interests by producing a collection of pseudo-classical epistles, *Athenian Letters, or the Epistolary Correspondence of an Agent of the King of Persia*, between 1741 and 1743. Birch, who had been granted a clerical living by Yorke's father, was engaged to see through the London press a private edition of about a dozen copies. This transaction evolved

---

[46] This friendship is discussed in the context of the Yorke-Grey coterie in Schellenberg, *Literary Coteries*, pp. 40–42.

(a)

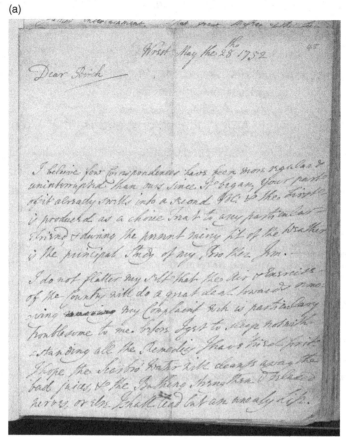

(b)

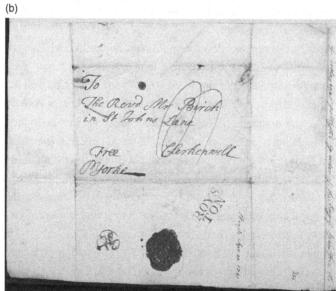

Figure 13 Two openings from folio volumes in the Hardwicke-Birch correspondence in the British Library: the first image is of BL Add MS 35396,

Caption for Figure 13 (cont.)

f. 24, the address page of Yorke to Birch, 20 Sept. 1741 (quoted later), with Birch's subsequent letter just visible behind; the second image is of Yorke to Birch, 28 May 1752, BL Add MS 35398, f. 45 (quoted later), again with Birch's next letter appearing behind.

into an engagement on Birch's part to send a weekly epistolary account of London literary (and political) news to Yorke during the seasons when the latter was in the country; the ensuing dialogue ended only with Birch's death in 1766.

Thus rooted in a patron-client relation, these letters are viewed by Markman Ellis as reflecting the seventeenth-century secretary's role, with "its mixture of trust, service and friendship";[47] indeed, we see them becoming the foundation of a friendship in the modern sense of a relationship characterized by egalitarian exchange, compatibility of interests, and companionship. While scholars have generally focused on the letters as a source of literary gossip, Yorke praises Birch as a gifted practitioner of the familiar letter genre. Rather than writing as a mere formality, "with you it is a relaxing of the mind in the most ingenuous way, communicating the fruits of one's studies, & speculations & repairing the loss of a Friends good Company in the most effectual manner." Birch in turn acknowledges that one dimension of Yorke's friendship is the prestige it brings (it is "a Friendship, which I feel the influence of in the kind Opinion entertain'd of me by others"), but he values it not only as "the Ornament" but also as "the Happiness of my Life." For Yorke, the unexpected death of Birch after a fall from his horse in January 1766 is marked as "a day I will always remember with grief, and will always honour."[48]

Both men show awareness of the correspondence as a cumulative text with its own structural logic, governing metaphors, and conventions. Thus Birch opens the annual cycle on June 29, 1751, upon Yorke's return from London to Wrest, with a self-conscious flourish:

> At the Entrance of the Eleventh Year of my Correspondences, the only Preface I shall use is the well known Observation, that quiet Times, tho' the best to live in, are most unfriendly to the Writer of them. But I have so great a Regard for the Peace of the World, that I shall be more contented to have my Letters neglected for their Emptiness or Insignificance, than to have the Occasions of filling them with Events ... arising from the Misery &

---

[47] Ellis, "Thomas Birch's 'Weekly Letter,'" p. 273.

[48] Yorke to Birch, 20 Sept. 1741, BL Add MS 35396, f. 22; Birch to Yorke, 23 Nov. 1741, BL Add MS 35396, ff. 42–43; Yorke's memorial to Birch is a Latin annotation to the last letter he had received from Birch, dated 4 Sept. 1765, BL Add. MS 35400, f. 300v.

Devastation of the Nations, ... I hope to see no other Wars, than of the Republic of Letters, a State, which is never like to enjoy a thorough Tranquillity, while the Appetite for Fame or Bread urges its Members to constant Hostilities.

A year later Yorke attests to the value of this chronicle of the Republic of Letters as retrospective entertainment: "I believe few Correspondences have been more regular & uninterrupted than ours since It began; your part of it already swells into a second Vol: & the First is produced as a choice Treat to any particular Friend, & during the present rainy fit of the Weather is the principal Study of my Brother Jem."[49]

Although Yorke remained the aristocratic amateur and Birch the energetic professional, there was clearly something in the former's function as reliable cheerleader ("Let me raise the dying flame before It quite expires, ... Is application necessary I will second it; Is Money wanting I will advance it, Is the Labor of Eyes demanded, I will at least share with You ye glorious Toil") that affirmed the value of Birch's labors. Above all, the two men shared what Yorke facetiously calls a "laudable Ardor for old Sacks, bad Hands, & dusty Bundles." Markman Ellis has described the pair's Whig historiography in general as driven by a "[high] regard for primary evidence," expressed in their "archival recovery of the correspondence of the officers of the state, secret service intelligence, small pamphlets and satires, and newsbooks and newspapers," used not only in their own research but also edited and published by them.[50] Dedication to documentary research also led to their working in tandem on such influential projects as the revival of the Royal Society (to which Yorke was elected in 1741 and for which Birch was secretary, 1752–65) and the establishment of the British Museum (Yorke chaired the parliamentary committee behind its founding, and both men served as trustees).

The significant socioeconomic gulf bridged by this productive collaboration is illustrated on one occasion when Yorke suggests that Birch is being taken advantage of by his publisher Andrew Millar and naively asserts that if his forthcoming edition of *The Memoirs of the Reign of Queen Elizabeth* (published 1754) were to be puffed properly, it would sell as well as a Henry Fielding or Charlotte Lennox novel. Birch's response is uncharacteristically testy:

You may judge of the Bargain, which I have made with Millar, & what better Terms I could expect from other Booksellers, from this short Estimate of the Expence, that the printing of the Sheets will amount to 98£, the paper to 81£,

---

[49] Birch to Yorke, 29 June 1751, BL Add. MS 35398, f. 1; Yorke to Birch, 28 May 1752, BL Add. MS 35398, f. 45.

[50] Ellis, "*The English Mercurie* Hoax," p. 114.

the binding of 500 Copies of the Volumes, in 4to, at 4s. a Book 100£ & advertisements & other incidental Charges to 10£, that is, 289£ in the whole. The Sale of which, computed at 18.s a Book, the highest price to the Booksellers, tho' sold to Gentlemen at a Guinea, will raise 450£, from which 289£, the Expence, being deducted, the Profit to be divided between the Author & Bookseller will be 161£, out of which the latter cannot be expected to allow 100 Guineas for the Copy, & at the same time run the risque of the whole.[51]

While a valuable account of mid-century trade economics in its own right, the dynamic context of explaining his professional life to an outsider leads Birch to adopt more forcefully than ever before the stance of a professional author whose expertise authorizes him to challenge his social superior's uninformed stereo-types about the avarice of the commercial book trade. As a cumulative, dialogic whole, then, this correspondence preserves not only London literary news but also the fashioning of an unusual social bond based on shared literary interests and historical values.

3.3 "Minds Are Free to Chuse Their Own Associates": Catherine Talbot and Jemima, Marchioness Grey

The documentary records left by another pair within the same social network, Catherine Talbot and Yorke's wife Jemima, demonstrate how familiar corres-pondence between educated women can evolve, not from patron-client business transactions to friendly intimacy, as in the case of Yorke and Birch, but from sociable reading to intellectual exchange and critical confidence. The fate of these records also illustrates the vulnerability of women's papers in the archival record. That a portion of the Talbot-Grey correspondence has been preserved reflects the enhanced survival rate of family papers housed in country estates: Grey's daughter Amabel, Baroness Lucas, transcribed her mother's correspond-ence after the latter's death, and these transcriptions passed to the Bedfordshire Records Office in the twentieth century as part of the Wrest Park (Lucas) archive. At the same time, the accidental destruction of Talbot's side of the correspondence mentioned earlier tells a different story from that of the care-fully collated and deposited Hardwicke-Birch correspondence. Mitigating this inequity is the fact that Birch's documentation habits extended to the writings of accomplished women; thus we owe those letters from Talbot to Grey that we do

---

[51] Birch to Yorke, 30 June 1753, f. 126, in response to Yorke to Birch, 28 June 1753, BL Add. MS 35398. According to the UK National Archives' historical currency converter, Millar's profit of £161 would have been the equivalent of about 4½ years' wages for a skilled tradesman in 1750. Birch had worked on the thousand-page publication for more than a year, including correction of proofs at a rate of ten hours a day for two months (Gunther, *Life of the Rev. Thomas Birch*, p. 48).

have to his copying a set of them, now held in the British Library as part of his correspondence.

Catherine Talbot (1721–70), the posthumous child of a clergyman, spent her life in the household of Thomas Secker, Bishop of Oxford and eventually Archbishop of Canterbury. As a girl, she acquired a reputation for learning and wit but became increasingly diffident about drawing attention to herself; despite several romantic attachments, she never married and succumbed to cancer at the age of forty-eight. Jemima Campbell (1722–97), heiress to the Duke of Kent, became mistress of Wrest and *suo jure* Marchioness Grey at her marriage in 1740. Formed in childhood, the Talbot-Grey relationship weathered their very different social destinies. As Grey writes in 1749:

> Your Friendship I have always thought one of my dearest and most valuable Blessings, & I may with much greater Reason than you can possibly do, join in looking back with Pleasure & Gratitude to its beginning, & rejoice that such Connexions are not always confin'd within a narrow Circle of the first Family-Acquaintance, but that Minds are free to chuse their own Associates, & that Ours were so early led by Providence to form an Interest & Attachment in each Other that will last with our Lives. For why should not we say *Friendships* as well as *Marriages are made in Heaven,* – they are often better worth it![52]

From the beginning, this union of minds was nurtured by shared reading; early exchanged notes refer to a love of multivolume romances as well as Greek and Roman classics and Sir Philip Sidney. A direct line can be traced between these youthful tastes and the two women's adult responses to contemporary literary events; Grey herself draws that connection when she speaks of weeping over the novel *Clarissa* just as the girls and their kittens once wept over the play *Celia*.[53] Grey's letters show the women building each other's critical confidence through common responses, with locutions such as "We follow'd your example, & amused ourselves upon the Road with David Simple [by Sarah Fielding]," frequently introducing incisive commentary on everything from Fielding's characterizations, to Madame de Sevigné's letters, contemporary political ballads, and John Locke's *Essay Concerning Human Understanding*.[54] Grey illustrates the function of such confidence building among women when she slyly confides the "*Disgracia*" of having a new, four-volume translation of Horace delivered to her while serving tea to a set of "Fine *Gem'men*," who she fears will look askance at her choice of reading material – "An English Translation is always one should think Unexceptionable, – but then it had Latin

---

[52] Grey to Talbot, 12 Oct. 1749, L30/9a/5, ff. 153–54.

[53] Grey to Talbot 28 Nov. 1747, L30/9a/5, ff. 42–46.

[54] Grey to Talbot 22 May 1744, L30/9a/3, ff. 107–8.

of One Side, & *which* I read you know may be doubtful." The tone is clearly facetious, but the "disgrace" can be described as such precisely because Grey's reader has experienced the same discomfort of being singled out as a learned woman.[55] While Grey's wide-ranging commentary should not be represented as always concerned with issues of gender directly, the safety of female friendship allows her to observe, for example, that while Pliny's letters portray him as a good family man, "I don't find how *Mrs. Pliny* (for all his charming Account of her & his Letters to her) could have any Share in [his Country-Life]."[56]

Grey repeatedly expresses appreciation to Talbot's affirmation of her critical judgments, like the recognition of Samuel Richardson's "Forte" as being "*Characters*, such as may be met with daily in the World, strongly & naturally described, & the Incidents in Common Life most affectingly told."[57] It has been argued that such exchanges led to some of the first extended critical responses to canonical literary publications of the period, including Richardson's *Clarissa* and Samuel Johnson's periodical *The Rambler* (1750–52).[58] That Talbot was fully engaged can be inferred from Grey's responses to her friend's critical positions; such dialogues were arguably the training ground for Talbot's most extended critical enterprise: her active, though carefully hidden, role as editor of Richardson's *Sir Charles Grandison*.[59]

Grey's frequent distance from Talbot is the subject of lament, here again presented in terms of shared reading:

> I am much pleased we have sympathised so much without knowing it; & that You too are studying Clarendon. . . .. Alas! Why should our Eyes travel over the same Pages & yet be at such a distance from One Another's! Why must we only see the same Words, & not be able to see what we wish so much for, – each Other![60]

If separation was painful to the two women, the handwritten records that resulted yield insights that would otherwise have been lost to the ephemeral medium of conversation. Thus this manuscript correspondence serves as a memorial to the strength of female friendship bonds, while allowing us to encounter the resistance of women to dominant narratives about their cultural roles. Fortunately, there remains enough of a manuscript witness to Catherine Talbot's and Jemima Grey's literary sociability to enable us to understand the

---

[55] In a journal kept during a June 1745 visit to Wrest, Talbot records her extreme discomfort at a group of unexpected guests who expect her to say clever things based on her "fame" as a "Bel Esprit" (11 June 1745, L30/106, n.p.).

[56] Grey to Talbot 18 Jan. [1745], L30/9a/4, ff. 30–32; Grey to Talbot 17 Jan. 1746, L30/9a/4, ff. 179–80.

[57] Grey to Talbot 28 Nov. 1747, L30/9a/5, ff. 42–46.   [58] Orchard, "Dr. Johnson on Trial."

[59] Schellenberg, "Catherine Talbot Translates Samuel Richardson."

[60] Grey to Talbot 7 Sept. 1742, L30/9a/3, f. 87.

crucial role familiar letters could play in the intellectual engagements of women.

3.4 "A Valuable Piece to Add to My Invaluable Collection": Elizabeth Montagu

Our final example, the correspondence of Elizabeth Montagu, reflects in its sheer bulk and variety the multiple, interconnected facets of her life; in 1780, Montagu wrote to a friend, "In the course of two posts I had letters from a Polish Prince, a great dealer in Cattle, one of the most distinguished of our Literati, my Northern Steward, a great Scotch Philosopher, my head Carpenter in Portman Square, the sweet Minstrel Dr Beattie, an artist at Birmingham, my Baillif at Sandleford & many characters between these extremes."[61] Born to a gentry family with more pedigree than wealth, Elizabeth Robinson (1718–1800) married a grandson of the Earl of Sandwich, Edward Montagu, in 1742, and eventually became manager of her husband's estates and coal mines, all of which she inherited from him in 1775. After her marriage, she actively sought out intellectual mentors and in the process formed the principal nucleus of those interconnected circles that became known as Bluestocking assemblies, hosting gatherings at her London residences on Hill Street and then Portman Square. As much valuable scholarship of the past two decades has shown, attending to the largely non-print phenomenon of Bluestocking sociability is crucial to an understanding of how mid- to late-eighteenth-century public culture worked; this entails grappling with the correspondences that cemented Bluestocking relationships and furthered their projects when members were apart.[62] This brief discussion cannot offer an overview of the entire Montagu correspondence; it will simply comment on her creation of highly crafted passages of description and reflection that she could then adapt and deploy from one epistolary context to another in a sophisticated process of authorial "versioning." While this term, adopted from software studies, is used in textual scholarship to refer to the practice of representing multiple versions of a text rather than privileging any one "authoritative" version (see Section 4), it is invoked here to describe Montagu's self-conscious methods as a practitioner of the familiar letter form.

In addition to an analysis of archiving methods used by letter recipients and, eventually, Montagu's household (when her letters were returned to her after the original recipients' deaths), Markman Ellis details evidence of Montagu's

---

[61] Montagu to Sir William Weller Pepys, 16 Nov. 1780, mo4061.

[62] See especially Eger, *Bluestockings: Women of Reason*, ch. 2; Guest, *Small Change*, "Introduction."

practice of having multiple copies made (likely by female companions or secretaries) of certain of her own letters, presumably so that she could circulate clusters of her correspondence.[63] As Yorke's sharing of Birch's weekly letters with his guests indicates, eighteenth-century letters were commonly read for entertainment within the circles of their recipients, but Ellis suggests further that this systematic copying, archiving, and circulation by Montagu as well as her correspondents marks her growing reputation as a notable epistolary author.[64] What he does not explore is the sorts of letters chosen for copying. The kind of showpiece passage just described is notable among them, indicating that Montagu is selecting for reproduction, and presumably for circulation, those letters in which her writing is at its most virtuosic. In the correlation between her production of such pieces and letters selected for circulation, the correspondence documents the development of Montagu's literary practice and the process by which her literary reputation was constructed.

Reflecting the period's appreciation of the familiar letter as a form requiring both skill and creativity, friends as early as 1745 describe Montagu's witty letters as artifacts they intend to save. Anne Donnellan writes of one description of the seaside at Southampton, "tis a valuable piece to add to my invaluable collection which I shall leave to posterity as a trophy that I had a friend who coud think so justly & so brightly, & in both ortouch the collections of Pope Swift &c."[65] A tour of Southampton in late summer 1747 elicits at least two such pieces: the second, a description of a tour including Southampton and Mount Bevis, country seat of Lord and Lady Peterborough, will be discussed briefly here. First, Montagu shows that she shares Donnellan's judgment by repurposing the Southampton seaside prospect from two years earlier. To Donnellan, Montagu had written,

> I think the Sea a most Glorious object; when one Considers the Tides, ruled by Bodies at a vast distance, the infinite Number of Creatures that are Contain'd in it, & how by wafting Ships in a swifter manner than any other we can have of transporting ourselves from place to Place, it Assists that intercourse between distant Nations that it should seem to prevent. how admirable! . . . all tast [*sic*] the benefits of that Commerce of which it is the Parent. (See Figure 14.)

---

[63] In some cases, copies seem also to have been made specifically for use in Matthew Montagu's edition of the letters; while the date of copy production often cannot be determined with certainty, these edition-related copies can frequently be identified by their correlation with changes to the originals found in the print edition.

[64] Ellis, "Letters, Organization, and the Archive," pp. 609–13, 629.

[65] Donnellan to Montagu, 11 July [1745], mo778.

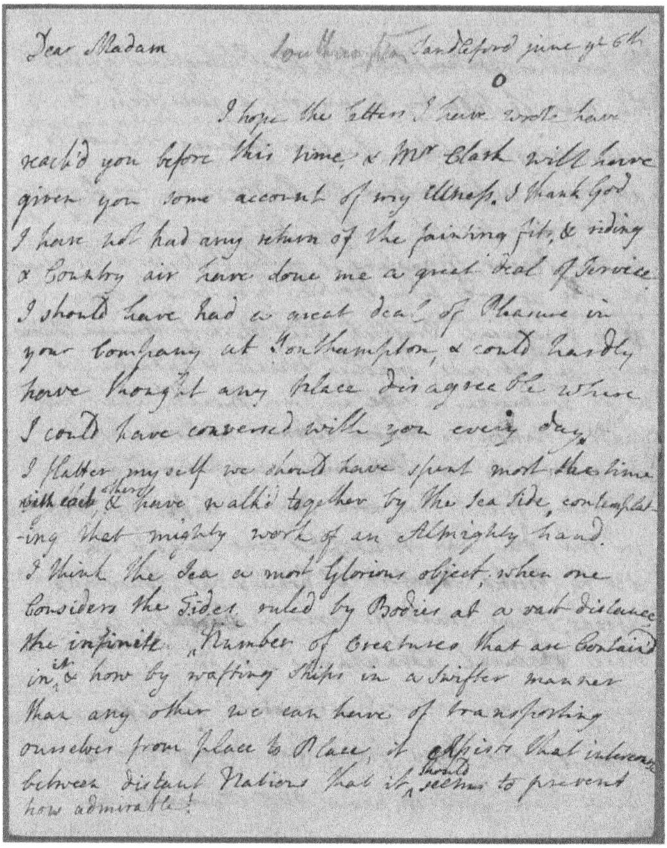

Figure 14 Montagu's 6 June 1745 letter to Anne Donnellan describing the sea at Southampton. Mo847, p. 1, Montagu Collection, The Huntington Library.

Now, to her clergyman cousin William Freind, who is teaching her Latin, Montagu distills the earlier two-page sentiment about the paradoxical nature of the sea into a few words – "I look upon the Sea as the greatest of Roads, & how finely is it contrived, that an unfirm Element which will not bear the foot, and seems a Barrier & hindrance to Commerce and Neighbourhood, should be the easiest of passages, & promote that intercourse of Nations which it seems to have forbidden" – before continuing with her description of Mount Bevis (Figure 15).

This pattern of repurposing, in condensed and pointed form, an initially diffuse reflection for the perusal of a (generally male) interlocutor whom Montagu is more anxious to impress continues with the Mount Bevis accounts. Montagu's sister Sarah serves as the addressee of the expansive and informal

(a)

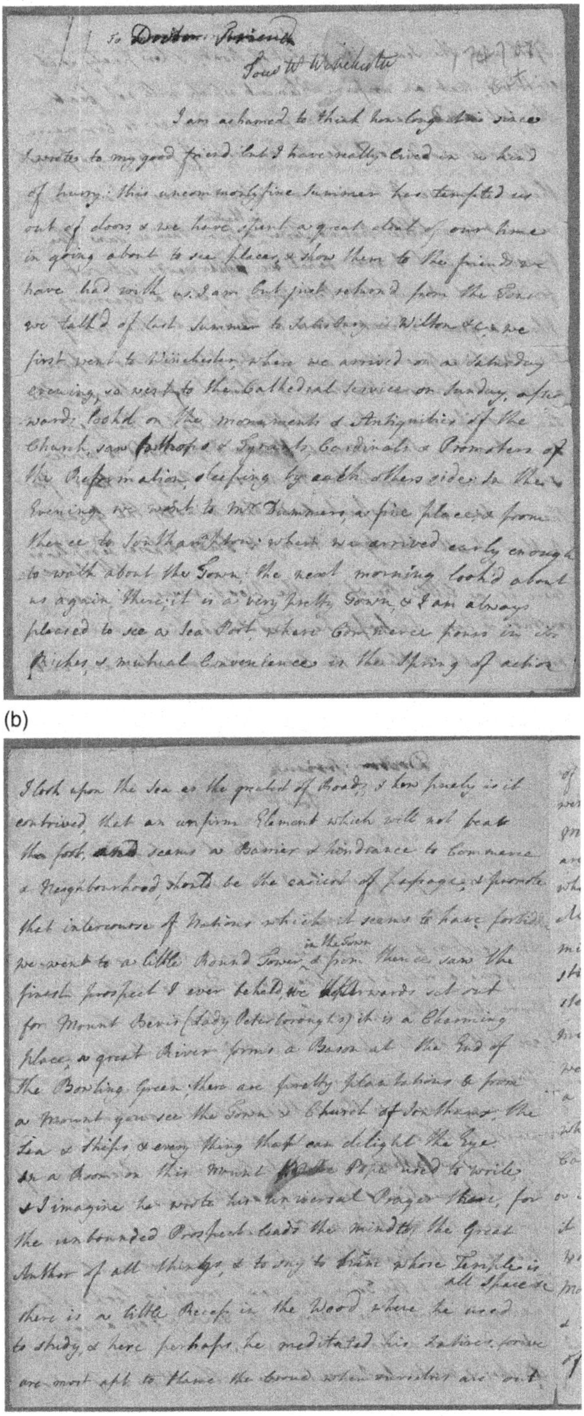

(b)

Figure 15 Montagu's c. Sept. 22, 1747 letter to William Freind, showing pp. 1–2 of the original letter describing the sea and Pope's writing spots at Mount Bevis

(c)

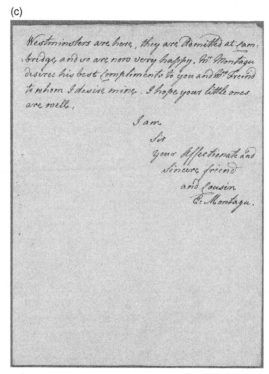

(d)

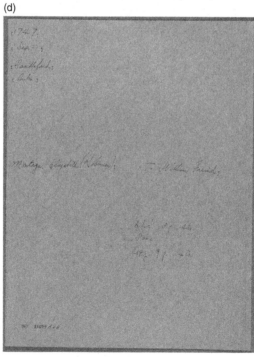

Figure 15 Cont

Caption for Figure 15 (cont.)

(with various notations by subsequent editors at the top of p. 1), the sign-off of the copied version, and the Huntington Library's blue folder in which the letter and copy are stored. Mo1039, Copy A pp. 1–2, Copy B p. 9, and blue archival folder, Montagu Collection, The Huntington Library.

"first drafts," while William Freind and the Duchess of Portland are addressed at the end of the sequence.[66] To her sister, Montagu offers a rather formless, paratactic sequence of reflections upon the poet Alexander Pope's connection to Mount Bevis:

> I sat on a Bench where Mr Pope used to study; then was carried to a Summer House which stands on a Mount & commands a fine Prospect: here Mr Pope used to write, & his Chair & Desk are sacredly kept; I cannot imagine how he could write satire in a place where every thing inspires pleasure & satisfaction: I cannot but think he wrote his Universal prayer here to him whose Temple is all space &c the boundless prospect might inspire it & the beauty of the place give the mind a turn of Gratitude. I never saw any Garden that pleased me so much as Mount Bevis, Ld Peterborough says in a letter to Pope I confess the lofty Sacharissa at Stow but am content with my own little Amoret, indeed he had Reason, Stow is a fine Court Lady much adornd & set off by art, Mount Bevis a Beauteous Rural Nymph whose Graces want no ornam^t whose dress indeed is well understood but to adorn wd be to encumber her & hide charms that art cannot improve.

We quote at length to illustrate how Montagu selects and sharpens her observations when she writes to Freind and the duchess later that month. The letter to the duchess reflects Montagu's former position as Portland's companion, valued for her liveliness and wit, whereas that addressed to Freind foregrounds elevated and abstract sententiousness. The latter version, the one Montagu selected for copying (and presumed circulation), minimizes scene setting in favor of a schematic contrast between Pope's forms of writing:

> In a Room on this Mount Pope used to write, and I imagine he wrote his Universal Prayer there, for the unbounded Prospect leads the mind to the Great Author of all things, ... there is a little Recess in the Wood, where he Used to study, and here perhaps he Meditated his Satires, for we are most apt to blame the Croud when ourselves are out of the Tumult.

---

[66] The sequence of extant letters is dated as follows: Scott is the addressee on 5 Sept. 1747 (mo5701), then Donnellan *c.* 20 Sept. (mo852), Montagu's sister-in-law Lady Jemima Medows 16 Sept. Freind *c.* 22 Sept. (mo1039), and the Duchess 22 Sept. (mo424).

The duchess, in turn, receives a letter that omits Pope's writings altogether, in favor of the passage on Lord Peterborough's words to Pope, now carefully set off by quotation marks so as to signal as Montagu's own a more succinct and authoritative rendering of the metaphoric contrast she originally produced for her sister: "for tho Stowe like a Court Beauty is adorn'd with art & ornamented with much expence; the Native Graces of Mount Bevis surprize & charm the beholder & have an effect that art can never reach."

Montagu shows herself to be similarly concerned to convey refined literariness in writing to another distant cousin and intellectual mentor, the poet and Christian polemicist Gilbert West, in 1755. Visiting her friends the Admiral and Frances Boscawen in Surrey, she writes versions of detailed landscape descriptions to her husband and sister, reflecting their interests as landowner and armchair traveler, respectively. To West, by contrast, Montagu chooses only to note that she has been busy "seeing places in the Neighbourhood," launching from a general description of pastoral scenes into an abstract meditation on Admiral Boscawen's relinquishment of such scenes, like the heroes of the *Odyssey,* "for the stern trade of War, the rough and treacherous element of the Sea, and all the incumbrances and embarrassment of a considerable command," motivated "to 'seek the bubble reputation even in the cannons [*sic*] Mouth.'" From here the author appropriates *King Lear*'s description of the "dreadful trade" of picking samphire on the cliffs to describe this "Method of gathering Laurels on the dangerous steeps and rocks of Ambition."[67] This highly literary and topical piece, written at the start of the Seven Years' War, is again preserved in a secretarial copy in the Montagu Collection, like a fair copy manuscript of a literary work. Whether or not Montagu had it circulated at the time, we do know that West himself copied, or had copied, many of Montagu's letters, circulating them to the likes of the Archbishop of Canterbury and the politician-poet George Lyttelton, later her intimate friend and a central figure in her Bluestocking circle. Ellis posits that Montagu-initiated copying occurs most commonly in correspondence with West, Lyttelton, and a third friend William Pulteney, the earl of Bath because these "established gentlemen of literary note" influenced Montagu to adopt "a practice peculiar to men of their status."[68] As the argument above has suggested, however, Montagu is not simply imitating but has long been pursuing and has been encouraged to pursue through the responses of her correspondents the construction of a literary reputation. This self-consciousness is reflected in the forms of textual production she chose, in

---

[67] Montagu to West, 27 July 1755 (mo6726).
[68] Ellis, "Letters, Organization, and the Archive," p. 629.

her versioning of texts, and in the circulation practices that facilitated and managed selective exposure.

This brief discussion of three correspondences models an approach to the familiar letter as something more than an assemblage of eyewitness documents. Reading these artifacts as material embodiments of literary sociability, we learn how literary identities such as historian, critic, and author were developed in a collaborative, dialogic process that allowed participants, over an extended period of time, to move beyond the apparent limitations of subordinate social status, expectations of female intellectual inferiority, and a lack of educational opportunity. At the same time, tracing their initial circulation gives us a glimpse of how familiar letters themselves functioned to establish social networks, articulate critical principles, and, simply, to entertain. Finally, the differing practices of collection applied to these correspondences, and the values that shaped those practices, serve as a challenge and a caution to the scholar who wishes to make use of such resources. Section 4 will address similar issues regarding the surviving manuscripts of literary authors whose reputations are founded primarily on their print publications.

4 Manuscript Circulation and Print Publication

For the eighteenth and early nineteenth centuries, we possess the archives of more literary authors than for previous periods, in part because more authors (and their friends, family members, publishers, and literary executors) made deliberate decisions to retain their literary manuscripts, and in part because their archives have been more likely to be preserved in the long term. With increasing quantities of these artifacts, it is possible to trace literary works through the processes of composition, revision, and publication, whether in scribal copies or print, though usually by consulting both. By carefully studying material artifacts including authorial drafts, fair copies, transcripts, corrected printed proofs, and print editions, as well authorial corrections made in print editions and correspondence, it is possible to track the process by which manuscripts circulated and were transformed into print, and to understand the interrelations between manuscript and print practices. Literary draft manuscripts of the period, particularly of works that were published in print by well-known authors, have traditionally been the purview of textual scholars, who have attended to the manuscripts as a means of generating an authoritative text for reading and scholarship. However, draft (and even fair copy) manuscripts of printed works can tell us more: about how authors compose and revise in handwritten documents; about how literary culture relies upon social networks for production, correction, and circulation; and about how authors reworked their writing for wider reader-ships both before and after its initial printing. This section examines manu-scripts of literary texts that were published in print to reflect upon these transformative processes, concluding with a brief consideration of the mech-anisms by which these documents have come to survive.

During the long eighteenth century, all literary works, even if the author had a clear plan to publish the composition, began as handwritten docu-ments. This fact has some important implications. It means that, unlike today, when it is possible to compose directly in word-processing software without ever putting pen to paper, creating a literary work in the eighteenth century was a physical process that left traces in ink or pencil on paper; these traces are available to us today if the writing surfaces survive and the ink remains legible. In addition, unlike today when there are many pro-cesses and instruments for writing, the practices and tools of writing in the eighteenth century were fairly standardized. This is not to say that when we examine a literary manuscript, we can readily and easily determine how and why it was made. Unlike printed books, which are usually addressed to the public and hence provide information to orient readers – in the form of titles, genre descriptions, authorial attributions, imprints identifying the place of publication and the book's manufacturers, and dates – literary manuscripts, usually prepared for readers who know what they are exam-ining, often provide none of this information. Often, to make sense of a manuscript and its paths of circulation, we need additional information, in the form of other manuscript and print witnesses, as well as external evidence such as correspondence between an author and publisher. This section examines three phases of what we might call the life cycle of literary manuscripts: their production, circulation, and, in some cases, publication in print (as not all literary manuscripts were published). Section 5 considers what happens to literary manuscripts after their origin-ally intended uses have passed, as they are preserved, taken into archives, and reproduced for subsequent generations.

4.1 Manuscript Production

Most literary manuscripts during the period were written on paper, a physical process described in more detail in Section 1 above. Short poems were regularly copied onto blank sheets and sent as enclosures in letters and were often circulated with no plan to publish them in print. As the discussion in Section 2 of Sarah Wilmot's notebooks illustrates, many poems were written to celebrate occasions – births or deaths, social and public events. Fair copies of these occasional poems would usually be sent to a recipient or recipients; sometimes these fair copies survive, but often the poem is known through other sources. For example, Anna Barbauld's thirty-six-line poem "To a little invisible being who is expected soon to become visible" was known until recently only through its posthumous publication, in *Works of Anna Laetitia Barbauld, With a Memoir* published by Barbauld's niece Lucy Aikin in 1825. In 1994, a manuscript copy was discovered in a collection called "Miscellaneous Extracts," with a note: "Sent to Mrs W Carr a short time before the birth of her first child"; Thomas William and Frances Carr were close friends of Barbauld, and the poem was probably written not before the birth of their first daughter, but their second, Frances Rebecca, born in June 1796, likely an error made by the writer of the note.[69] As Section 2 explains, it was a common practice to collect poems (and other "extracts") in blank paper-books, and this one has nine poems by Barbauld as well as many by other poets; it is undated and unsigned and so the creator of the collection is unknown. Although the original copy of "To a little invisible being" Barbauld sent to Mrs. W. Carr does not survive, we can piece together its likely transmission through the printed and manuscript copies that do. Collections of manuscript poems, as well as letters and other unpublished writing, were often posthumously published, with family members or close associates of the deceased author acting as editors. These publications frequently took the form of memorials to the dead as well as attempts to establish a canon of works for the author. With Aikin's publication of her aunt's *Works of Anna Laetitia Barbauld, With a Memoir*, and also the edited collection of educational writing, *A Legacy for Young Ladies*, thirty-five of Barbauld's verse and prose pieces were printed for the first time.[70]

Fiction was often, as we will see in this section, written in notebooks. Jane Austen handmade small booklets for drafting her fiction. It has been speculated that she made these "by cutting down half sheets of 'post' writing paper, 385 x 480 mm, to form quires of up to eight leaves (16 pages) which could then be assembled inside one another to make fatter booklets," which may have been bound together with a central pin or thread.[71] According to her nephew, Austen "was careful that her occupation should not be suspected by servants, or visitors, or any persons beyond her own family party. She wrote upon small sheets of paper which could easily be put away, or covered with a piece of blotting paper."[72] And the booklets she made *are* small: the surviving *Persuasion* notebook measures 6.1 x 3.5 inches (155 x 90 mm); the height of iPhone 11, which is only slightly narrower. Austen made these booklets to serve her

---

[69] From McCarthy's private collection; McCarthy, *Poems*, p. 212.
[70] McCarthy, *Collected Works*, p. xxii.
[71] Headnote, Sanditon, *Jane Austen's Fiction Manuscripts*.   [72] Austen-Leigh, *Memoir*, p. 96.

immediate purpose of drafting her fiction and for delivery of the manuscript to the publisher and then printer. The only extant writing from a print novel by Austen are the two canceled chapters of her final finished novel *Persuasion*, which survive in a gathering of sixteen leaves. Sometime between July 18 and August 6, 1816, Austen rewrote the ending by canceling the two originally drafted chapters and substituting three new chapters, which were published as the ending to the novel after her death in 1817. We can identify the surviving manuscript as an earlier version by the dates that appear on the manuscript (it is dated in three places: "July 8" at the top right-hand corner of the first leaf; "July 16 | 1816" at the bottom right-hand corner of what would be page 27; and "July 18. – 1816" at the bottom right-hand corner of what would be page 28).[73] We know that the new ending was written in July and August because of a memorandum, written by Austen's sister Cassandra, setting out the composition dates of the novels.[74]

Austen made use of another kind of notebook, purchased directly from stationers, to select, copy, and collect her juvenile writing, which, with self-conscious and ironic pomp she labeled "Volume the First," "Volume the Second," and "Volume the Third." Although there are some similarities between the second and third notebooks, experts believe that the three were made by different bookbinders, and so were possibly bought at different times.[75] Although the stories for the most part appear to be transcribed from other manuscripts that have not survived, and some dates are included in individual pieces, it is not clear if these are dates of original composition or of transcription. A further complication is that there is evidence of Austen copying, revising and possibly even drafting within the notebooks, blurring the lines between the volumes as fair copies and drafts.[76] Manuscript notebooks could be added to over time, and could easily accommodate the contributions of others as well as sketches and drawings (adding illustrations to printed books was more complex, as printing letterpress and printing engraved images required the use of different technologies). In "Volume the Second," Cassandra created watercolor roundel portraits as headers to each chapter in her mock "History of England" (Figure 16); and in "Volume the Third," we find attempted endings of two early novels Austen left unfinished (*Evelyn* and *Catharine, or the Bower*) by Austen's nephew and niece.[77] Notebooks allowed Austen to preserve her childhood writing and were also useful ground for experimentation and collaboration.

---

[73] Headnote, *Persuasion*, *Jane Austen's Fiction Manuscripts*.
[74] Morgan Library, MA 2911.12.
[75] Conservation Report, Volume the Third, *Jane Austen's Fiction Manuscripts*.
[76] Sabor, *Juvenilia*, p. xxxii.   [77] Sabor, *Juvenilia*, pp. xxxi–xxxii.

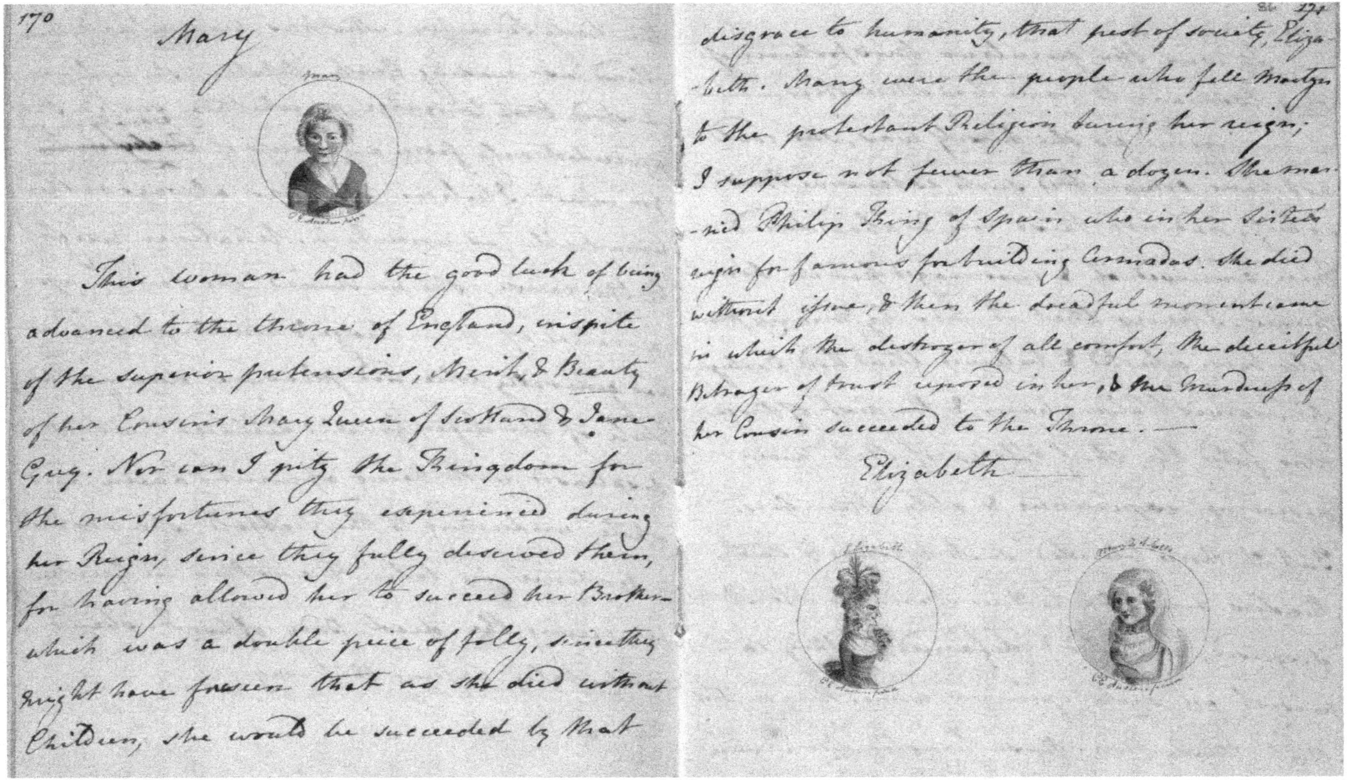

Mary

This woman had the good luck of being
advanced to the throne of England, inspite
of the superior pretensions, Merit & Beauty
of her Cousins Mary Queen of Scotland & James
of her Cousins Mary Queen of Scotland & James.
Nor can I pity the Kingdom for
the misfortunes they experienced during
her Reign, since they fully deserved them,
for having allowed her to succeed her Brother—
which was a double peice of folly, since they
might have foreseen that as she died without
Children, she would be succeeded by that

disgrace to humanity, that pest of society, Eliza:
-beth. Many were the people who fell Martyrs
to the protestant Religion during her reign;
I suppose not fewer than a dozen. She was
and Philip King of Spain, she wrote letters
signify for permanent purpose during her time,
released upon—& then the dreadful circumstances
in which the destroyer of all property, the destroyer
Stuart of trust reposed in her, & Mr Whitaker
to Queen succeeds to the Throne—

Elizabeth.

Figure 16 Jane and Cassandra Austen, "History of England," Volume the First, British Library, Add MS 59874.

One of Dorothy Wordsworth's notebooks, known as her "Commonplace Book," similarly demonstrates how notebooks could be used for a variety of purposes: to draft, revise, and fair copy her own poems and to copy poems and prose from other sources.[78] Wordsworth also uses the notebook to paste loose sheets of copies of her poems and others. For example, she made a fair copy of her poem to her niece, "To Dora Wordsworth," on a single sheet of paper that she pastes into the notebook alongside a draft of the same poem, titled "Lines intended for my Niece's Album." The fair copy includes a note that it was "Transcribed by S.H.," or Sara Hutchinson, the sister of William Wordsworth's wife Mary. The transcription is dated June 1832, a month after the date on the draft. The addition of the initials "W.W." under the note "Transcribed by S.H." seems to indicate that the transcription was added by William Wordsworth, such that the manuscript poem had at least three readers (including we must presume the addressee, Dora Wordsworth). In Figure 17, we see the pasting of the fair copy opposite the last three stanzas of the draft. By attaching the loose sheet fair copy next to the draft, Dorothy archives two documentary witnesses to the poem; in so doing, she records its textual transmission and the social circulation of the poem.

A label on this notebook indicates that it was purchased at a bookseller and binder known as GRISET FILS AÎNÉ in Boulogne Sur Mer, in Northern France, which Wordsworth visited for an extended period with her brother and sister-in-law in 1820. Notebooks like this one, with a durable, hardback cover could provide protection for the contents and could make it easier to store with other books. Further, notebooks allow for additional materials (such as described earlier) to be pasted or filed into or between their pages, thus enabling the notebook to serve an archival function. As with Austen's notebooks, we find evidence of both fair copying and revising, disrupting any tidy division between drafts and fair copies and demonstrating the complex nature of many manuscript notebooks. Wordsworth's notebook is also filled from both ends, another flexible feature of the notebook form.

4.2 Manuscript Circulation

Literary manuscripts can provide evidence of social circulation, allowing us to reconstruct the flow of literary texts, the practices used to transmit them, and the reception of these works. It is important to recognize that there were varying patterns by which manuscripts circulated. In the cases of the domestic and social poetry of Anna Barbauld, Sarah Wilmot, and Dorothy Wordsworth, as well as Jane Austen's juvenilia, publication in print did not take place until long after

---

[78] Dove Cottage MS 120, Wordsworth Trust.

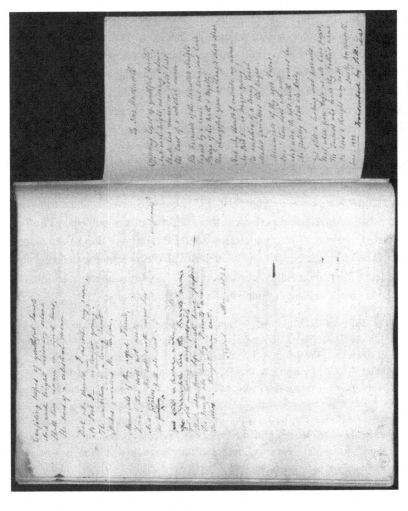

Figure 17 Dorothy Wordsworth, "Lines intended for my Niece's Album," "To Dora Wordsworth," Wordsworth Trust DCMS 120.23, f. 28ʳ, 120.24, inserted between ff. 28–29.

the deaths of the authors (indeed, Wilmot's poetry has yet to be printed). In other instances, manuscript circulation could precede print. Often, as is the case with the surviving manuscript of Austen's *Persuasion*, publication in print was intended by the author; in other cases, such as Thomas Gray's famous *Elegy Written in a Country Churchyard*, print publication seems to have been a consequence of the poem's wide circulation in manuscript. First composed in 1750, the *Elegy* was published in a quarto pamphlet by Robert Dodsley on February 15, 1751. The earliest manuscript version of the poem in Gray's hand (also known as an autograph or holograph, that is, written in the hand of the creator of the text) is held by Eton College, where the poem is titled "Stanza's, wrote in a Country Church-Yard." The second manuscript witness is found in a letter Gray sent to his friend Thomas Wharton on December 18, 1750; the third is in Gray's commonplace book, held at Pembroke College, Cambridge, where Gray lived from 1756 to 1771.[79] We also know that Gray sent another copy to Horace Walpole on June 12, 1750, though this copy does not survive. Both Wharton and Walpole were entranced by the poem, and they passed it around in manuscript and allowed copies to be taken, resulting in widespread circulation.

As a consequence, on February 10, 1751, Gray received a letter from the *Magazine of Magazines*, a periodical that collected pieces published in other periodicals or gleaned from manuscript sources, informing him of the magazine's plan to print the poem. Gray's letter to Walpole, in response to the receipt of this letter, written on either February 11 or 12, is worth quoting at length, for it explains Gray's decision to publish the poem immediately:

> [The editors of the *Magazine of Magazines*] tell me, that an *ingenious* Poem, call'd, *Reflections* in a Country-Churchyard, has been communicated to them, wch they are printing forthwith: that they are inform'd, that the *excellent* Author of it is I by name, & that they beg not only his *Indulgence*, but the *Honor of his Correspondence*, &c: as I am not at all disposed to be either so indulgent, or so correspondent, as they desire; I have but one bad Way left to escape the Honour they would inflict upon me. & therefore am obliged to desire you would make Dodsley print it immediately (wch may be done in less than a Week's time) from your Copy, but without my Name, in what Form is most convenient for him, but in his best Paper & Character. ... if he would add a Line or two to say it came into his Hands by Accident, I should like it better.[80]

From Gray's response, it is apparent that manuscript circulation could be so extensive as to force an author's hand. It is also worth remarking that Gray

---

[79] Huber, Alexander, ed. "Finding Aid Results." *Thomas Gray Archive*, Dec. 2, 2020. Retrieved from www.thomasgray.org/cgibin/findaid.cgi?ead=grayt.ead.0001&collection=poems&work=elcc

[80] Gray, Thomas. "Thomas Gray to Horace Walpole [11 or 12 February 1751]." *Thomas Gray Archive*, Dec. 2, 2020. Retrieved from www.thomasgray.org/cgi-bin/display.cgi?text=tgal0178>

wished for the poem to be described as having come into Dodsley's "Hands by Accident," a very common authorial fiction that Dodsley, writing as "The Editor" in the "Advertisement" to the first edition in quarto published on February 15, 1751, repeats, though he also offers a more truthful account of the poem's extensive circulation in manuscript:

> The following POEM came into my Hands by Accident, if the general Approbation with which this little Piece has been spread, may be call'd by so slight a Term as Accident. It is this Approbation which makes it unnecessary for me to make any Apology but to the Author: As he cannot but feel some Satisfaction in having pleas'd so many Readers already, I flatter myself he will forgive my communicating that Pleasure to many more.[81]

Dodsley maintained Gray's anonymity, but the *Magazine of Magazines*, in its February issue, printed the day after Dodsley's quarto edition appeared, did not, introducing "STANZA's *written in a Country Church-yard*" as "a fine copy of verses, by the very ingenious Mr Gray, of *Peter-house, Cambridge.*"[82] The poem was an immediate success, repeatedly reprinted in magazines; more consequentially, Dodsley's quarto was printed in five editions by the end of the year. An instant classic, the poem became one of the most revered of the eighteenth century.

Gray's "Elegy" is an example of what Peter Stallybrass has described as manuscript circulation prompting or compelling print publication; it also demonstrates how print could initiate even more copying, as the poem continued to be copied after its many appearances in print.[83] There are dozens of known transcripts of the poem in the decades postdating its first publication, found in commonplace books and miscellanies, such as those described in Section 2 and earlier in this section. The example of Gray's "Elegy" points to the importance of examining manuscript copies dated even after a poem has circulated extensively in print. An example of a collection of manuscript poetry that includes texts of poems from both manuscript and print sources and also includes print copies of the poems is found in George Keats's notebook gathering together various autograph manuscripts made by John Keats, George's copies of his brother's poems made from other manuscript copies, newspaper printings of his brother's poems, and copies of poems written about the poet. The notebook

---

[81] Gray, Thomas. *An elegy wrote in a country church yard.* Printed for R. Dodsley in Pall-Mall; and sold by M. Cooper in Pater-Noster-Row, [1751]. *Eighteenth Century Collections Online.* Retrieved from link.gale.com/apps/doc/CW0114140028/ECCO?u=sfu_z39&sid=bookmark-ECCO&xid=801b71cb&pg=2.

[82] "STANZA'S Written in a Country Church-Yard." *The Magazine of Magazines* (1751): 160–1. *ProQuest.*

[83] Stallybrass, "Printing."

presents evidence of the circulation of literary manuscripts, still within a family but across large distances. George and his wife, Georgiana, moved to America in 1818; after their migration, John regularly sent his brother letters in which he enclosed copies of his poems. George kept a notebook in which he included autograph copies John sent him of three poems ("The Pot of Basil," "Lines on the Mermaid Tavern," "Eve of St. Mark"). George also made copies of his brother's poems from autographs he had received that have not survived; it is surmised that these were based on autograph copies and not from printed editions, as the versions copied in the notebook contain variants that do not occur in print. Figure 18 shows the page onto which George copied the final stanzas of "To Autumn," discussed further in the following section (see

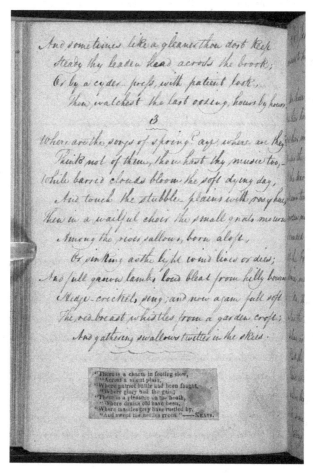

Figure 18 Poems by John Keats, Transcribed by George Keats. British Library Egerton MS 2780. f.58 v.

Figure 24). At the bottom of the page, George pasted a print clipping of John's poem "There is a charm in footing slow." Collections like George Keats's and those containing copies of Gray's "Elegy" survive to provide important reminders that print was not conceived of as replacing manuscript, and that both intimates of the poets and those without a personal connection collected and remade the poems as part of their own collections.

Printed poetry could be subject to more elaborate treatment than we see in George Keats's notebook, as we find in Williams Blake's extra-illustrated copy of Gray's poems, commissioned by Blake's friend the sculptor John Flaxman as a present for his wife, Ann, in 1797–8. Blake dismantled a letterpress edition of *Poems by Mr Gray*, published by John Murray in 1790, and mounted the letterpress into windows cut into larger sheets of paper.[84] Echoing medieval illuminated manuscripts, where handwritten text placed in a central window is surrounded by colored designs, Blake has enfolded the letterpress of Gray's poems with vibrant designs in pen, ink, and watercolor, bringing to life the scenes described. In Figure 19, we see Blake's rendering of "the harvest to the sickle yield[ing]" from the "Elegy," a monumental vision of agricultural labor that matches the poem's idealized description of rural life. The illustrated book of fifty-eight leaves was kept by the Flaxmans until 1828, when it was gifted by William Beckford to his younger daughter and was kept within that family until 1966. Blake's personalized copy of Gray's poems thus demonstrates how a commercially produced printed book could, through extra-illustration, be restored to the realm of private circulation.

4.3 Manuscript and the Printing Process

The survival of literary manuscripts of works intended for print is uneven in the long eighteenth century, as it was routine practice for printers to destroy the copy they used after the type had been set. Whereas with poetry, it was often the case that copies would have been shared prior to publication, ensuring the survival of some poetic manuscripts; with fiction, often all drafts and printer's copies were discarded. There are some notable exceptions to this general rule, however, and these extant fiction manuscripts provide fascinating opportunities for scholars seeking to learn about how authors prepared their manuscripts to send to the printing house, and about printing house practices.[85] Laurence Sterne's manuscript of the first volume of *A Sentimental Journey through France and Italy* first published in 1765, is a case in point, as one of the earliest surviving copies of an English novel in its creator's handwriting. The

---

[84] "Copy Information," www.blakearchive.org/copy/but335.1?descId=but335.1.wc.01
[85] See Havens, *Revising the Eighteenth-Century Novel*.

Figure 19 William Blake, *The Poems of Thomas* Gray, Design 109, "Elegy Written in a Country Church-Yard," between 1797 and 1798, Yale Centre for British Art, Paul Mellon Collection, B1992.8.11(55).

circumstances of and reasons for the survival of this manuscript are unknown, but it appears to have been a printer's copy, that is, the copy from which the type was set. The manuscript for the novel's second volume was sent to another printer, and as is consistent with usual practice, it does not survive. Melvyn New and W. G. Day, editors of the authoritative scholarly edition of *A Sentimental Journey*, have exhaustively studied the manuscript, and their analysis sheds light on what we can learn, about both authorial and printing practices, from a manuscript like Sterne's that reflects the near final intentions of the author.

New and Day note "that all claims to a Shandean sort of writing [referencing the outlandish narrator of Sterne's first novel], whereby words come as the spontaneous outpouring of exuberant spirits, are an illusion created by Sterne's narrators (and commentators)."[86] Although a mostly fair copy, there are more than five hundred additions and deletions to this final manuscript, demonstrating that Sterne reworked his prose, painstakingly refining and revising the final version. Other literary manuscripts of the period similarly contradict Romantic ideas about authorial genius that were emerging during the period, crystallized in statements like William Wordsworth's that "all good poetry is the spontaneous overflow of powerful feelings," a myth not exclusive to poetry, for Jane Austen's brother, Henry, insisted that "everything came finished from her pen."[87] Even the most cursory examination of a working manuscript by Wordsworth, or Austen, or Sterne reveals that writing was a product of continual revision and laborious effort.

From Sterne's manuscript, it is also possible to make inferences about how literary manuscripts were used in the printing process. Given the extent of the corrections and alterations, it is plain that printers were used to encountering and deciphering heavily marked-up manuscripts. Furthermore, a comparison of the manuscript and the first print edition reveals that Sterne must have corrected the typeset proofs (the first sheets printed, which would be corrected in the printing house and also often by the author or their surrogate). We know this because Sterne made additional changes in the first edition that are not in the manuscript. For example, in the manuscript the word "string" appears, but it has been changed for "cord" in the first edition, a change that, though slight, would not have been initiated by the printer.[88] From these sorts of changes, we may infer that Sterne was involved in seeing his work through the press, meaning that he was on hand to correct proofs. Austen also came to London in the 1810s for the express purpose of seeing her novels through the press, engaging in the same process of correction as Sterne in 1765.

4.4 The Manuscript Lifecycle

The few instances where we have more complete manuscript evidence allow for a more continuous tracing of the process from composition through to publication. This is the case with Mary Shelley's novel *Frankenstein*, where we have both parts of the original draft and fair copy manuscripts: there are two surviving draft notebooks, containing 87 percent of the finished novel, and two surviving fair copy notebooks of the likely original eleven, representing 12 percent of the completed novel.[89] The draft manuscript provides a material basis

---

[86] Sterne, *Sentimental*, p. xxxii.

[87] Wordsworth, "Preface," p. 744; Austen, 'Biographical,' p. xvi.

[88] Sterne, *Sentimental*, p. xxxi.   [89] Robinson, *Frankenstein*, p. 7.

for understanding Mary's compositional processes and her literary collaboration with her husband Percy Shelley. According to the editor of the notebooks,
Charles Robinson,

> There are times in the manuscript when you can actually "see" MWS and
> PBS at work on the Notebooks at the same time, possibly sitting side by side
> and using the same pen and ink to draft the novel and at the same time to enter
> corrections. We know from Sophia Stacey that in Florence PBS "at night has
> a little table with pen and ink, she [MWS] the same" . . . apparently, these
> were portable writing desks that allowed the two Shelleys to work near each
> other in their room at night.[90]

We can glimpse Robinson's vision of the Shelleys in Figure 20, which repro-
duces a page from chapter two of the first draft *Frankenstein* notebook. Percy

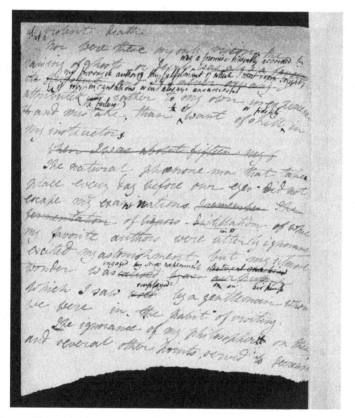

Figure 20 Mary Shelley (with Percy Shelley's revisions), Frankenstein
Notebook, Bodleian Library, MS. Abinger c. 56

[90] Robinson, *Frankenstein*, p. lxx.

Shelley's cancellations and additions are visible in a darker ink to Mary Shelley's original draft in a lighter ink; given the nature of his revisions, we can infer they came after Mary had written her words. We do not have the fair copy that relates to this section of the draft, so to further grasp the sequence of revisions, we must compare the textual versions in this manuscript with the first print edition. A study of these versions helps us piece together the creative and, in this case, collaborative processes by which a work of fiction was readied for print.

Percy's emendations to this paragraph are substantial, and to study them we present two methods for transcribing a draft manuscript. First is the diplomatic transcription made by Robinson, who has done the most to disentangle Mary's and Percy's contributions. A diplomatic transcription seeks to reproduce the way the words and marks appear on the manuscript, showing all cancellations and interlinear additions and attempting to replicate their positioning in the original. Robinson's transcription shows Mary Shelley's hand in roman font, Percy Shelley's in italic.

> Nor were these my only visions, the
> *was a promise liberally accorded by*
> raising of ghosts or devils ∧ ~~was also a favour~~
> *my favourite authors; the fulfilment of which I most eagerly sought;*
> ~~its pursuit~~ and ~~If I never say any~~
> *& if my incantations were always unsuccessful*
> attributed ~~it~~ rather to my own inexperience
> *the failure   to a   or fidelity*
> ~~th~~ and mistake, than ∧ want of skill ∧ in
> my instructors.[91]

Diplomatic transcription, particularly of such a complex set of changes, has it limits. We can see the extent of Percy Shelley's changes, but it may be easier to analyze them by separating out the two versions that are legible in the manuscript, as follows: (1) Mary Shelley's original draft in lighter ink, (2) the revised draft with Percy's changes in darker ink, and (3) the first print edition of 1818. The underlining denotes significant changes between the current and previous version in what might be considered a versioning model of textual change.

> (1) Mary Shelley's original draft [40 words]
> Nor were these my only visions, the raising of ghosts or devils was also a favourite pursuit and If I never saw any attributed it rather to my own inexperience and mistake than want of skill in my instructor.

---

[91] Robinson, *Frankenstein*, pp. 22–23. Every effort has been made to replicate Robinson's transcription as closely as possible.

(2) Mary Shelley's draft, with Percy Shelley's revisions [57 words]

Nor were these my only visions, the raising of ghosts or devils was <u>a promise</u> <u>liberally accorded by my favourite authors; the fulfilment of which I most</u> <u>eagerly sought; & if my incantations were always unsuccessful</u> attributed <u>the</u> <u>failure</u> rather to my own inexperience and mistake, than <u>to a</u> want of skill <u>or</u> <u>fidelity</u> in my instructors.

(3) First print edition (1818) [57 words]

Nor were these my only visions. <u>T</u>he raising of ghosts or devils was a promise liberally accorded by my favourite authors, the fulfillment of which I most eagerly sought; and if my incantations were always unsuccess-ful,<u> I</u> attributed the failure rather to my own inexperience and mistake, than to a want of skill or fidelity in my instructors.

Both of these notation systems reveal that there were only modest changes between Percy Shelley's corrected manuscript version and the first print edition, as it would seem Mary Shelley accepted most of his changes. The only new changes are that the first and second clauses are divided into sentences, and a second "I" is added, which may have been prompted by the need for clarity given Percy's revisions to the draft. It is entirely possible these changes were made by the printer as opposed to Percy or Mary in correcting proofs; as we do not have the fair copy manuscript for this section of the draft, we cannot determine for certain who initiated these changes.

The most significant revisions are those reflected in the two manuscript stages, that is, in the changes Percy Shelley made on the manuscript draft. Instead of the "raising of ghosts or devils" simply being described as "a favourite pursuit," the origin of this pursuit, in writing by Victor Frankenstein's "favourite authors," is elaborated; the desire for these pursuits is emphasized ("the fulfilment of which I most eagerly sought"); instead of the more prosaic statement about the failure to raise these ghosts, "and If I never saw any [visions]," we have the more descrip-tive and poetic "& if my incantations were always unsuccessful"; and rather than laying the blame for his lack of success on "want of skill in my instructor," Percy offers the more formal and circumlocutory, "to a want of skill or fidelity in my instructors." As Anne Mellor has astutely observed, Percy Shelley was "respon-sible for much of the most inflated rhetoric in the text."[92]

Many commentators, however, have tended to misunderstand the manu-script evidence, giving either more or less credit to Percy Shelley than is warranted because they were unable to decipher the different hands and had not undertaken a comprehensive survey of the manuscript evidence. Robinson's exhaustive study of the manuscript and his meticulous attributions have done much to correct the record and quell the considerable controversy

---

[92] Mellor, *Mary Shelley*, p. 62.

that has surrounded the composition of the novel. He quantifies Percy Shelley's contributions of around 4,000 words to the 72,000-word novel, and identifies precisely what his contributions were, line by line, word for word, so that others may assess their significance and meaning. He notes that the misreading of previous scholars "is a reminder of just how important a manuscript is to literary analysis."[93] He concludes, as do most scholars of the manuscript, that Mary Shelley was the primary author and intellectual force behind the novel, but that Percy played an essential role in shaping it. Nevertheless, a very few have persisted in claims that Percy Shelley's influence was considerable, an interpretation that discounts the evidence of Mary Shelley's handwriting through the assertion that she took down the draft to Percy's dictation, a supposition that is based on the belief that a nineteen-year-old girl without a formal education could not have written the novel. There are also some who accept that Mary Shelley was responsible for the words that appear in her hand but suggest that Percy is entitled to collaborator status for his work of revision. It bears mentioning that rarely (if ever) is the authorship of holograph manuscripts by men challenged, and rarely are there pleas for the women they worked with to receive authorial credit. In this way, literary manuscripts, when they survive, have an important role to play in questions of attribution, authorship, and collaboration; at the same time, even when the manuscripts do exist and are subject to scrupulous scholarly assessment, false assumptions and biases can impact their interpretation.

The notebooks that were used to create a fair or near-fair copy from the draft were likely the copy that was sent to prospective publishers. We know that a manuscript copy was sent to at least two (John Murray, Charles Ollier) and possibly a third unknown publisher, before it was sent to and accepted by James Lackington.[94] John Murray, who rejected the manuscript, complained about his struggle to keep track of the multitude of manuscripts he was receiving for consideration and created a rejection ledger as a means of keeping track of the manuscripts his firm had received and their return. On the first page of this ledger (Figure 21), there is an entry from June 17, 1817, that records the rejection of *Frankenstein, or [the] Modern Prometheus*, 3 vols., returned (denoted with an "R") on June 14 to one H. Smith, a pseudonym that must have been used by Percy Shelley who, in seeking to sell his wife's novel, wished to keep her authorship (as well as his relation to her) unknown. Once James Lackington agreed to publish the novel, the fair copy notebooks would have been sent to the printers to set the type. We know that the two surviving fair copy notebooks were used as printer's copies by the presence of ink fingerprints,

---

[93] Robinson, *Frankenstein*, p. lxix.   [94] Robinson, *Frankenstein*, pp. lxxxv–lxxxix.

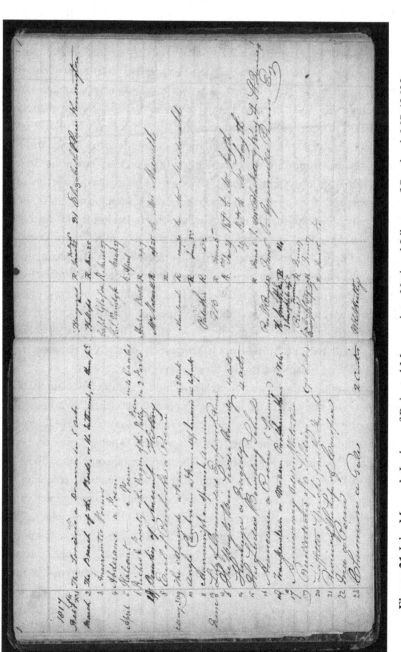

Figure 21 John Murray's Ledger of Rejected Manuscripts, National Library of Scotland, MS 42632.

compositor initials, folds, and other notations on the manuscript.[95] As is the case of the first volume of Laurence Sterne's manuscript of *A Sentimental Journey*, the printer would also have disbound the notebooks for the printing process.

We do not know why some of the fair copy and more of the draft of *Frankenstein* survive, in the same way we do not know why Sterne's manuscript of the first volume of *Sentimental Journey* was saved, though perhaps it was due to an unusual intervention of the printer, possibly a consequence of Sterne's wildly popular first novel, *Tristram Shandy*. Usually we trace preservation of literary manuscripts to family members who wished to keep them as mementos of their loved ones. We know that Jane Austen or a family member, likely Cassandra, decided to save the manuscript of the two discarded *Persuasion* chapters, possibly because they reflect the significant transformation of Austen's original ending. A note in Cassandra's hand on a strip of paper pasted across the final leaf – "The contents of this Drawer | for Anna" – indicates the manuscript was to be bequeathed to her niece, Anna Lefroy, suggesting its ongoing value within the family.[96] As discussed in the next section, Austen's literary manuscripts were sufficiently prized by her heirs to be kept safely until they had acquired some monetary value and were sold at auction. George Keats, as we have seen, performed the same function of conserving his brother's manuscripts until they became of interest to collectors. In Dorothy Wordsworth's case, her manuscripts were always valued within her family circle and, because her contributions to the family's literary economy were always recognized, her notebooks were preserved alongside those that feature her brother's poetry (as well as the many notebooks in which they are intermingled). It helped as well that the Wordsworths lived for many decades in one home, and that Wordsworth's celebrity was achieved during his (and his sister's) very long lifetimes. Carrying forward this section's discussion of the afterlives of literary manuscripts, Section 5 considers how literary manuscripts survived until the period in which they were taken into institutional repositories (or acquired by private collectors) and explores how we can both identify and understand the layers of meaning that have been added to literary artifacts over time.

5 Remediating the Manuscript Record

Most of us encounter literary manuscripts dating from the long eighteenth century in mediated forms. If we are fortunate enough to examine a literary manuscript in person, we almost always do so in libraries or archives. This

---

[95] Robinson, *Frankenstein*, pp. xlv; lxxv.
[96] Headnote, Persuasion, *Jane Austen's Fiction Manuscripts*.

means that our engagement with the artifact is inevitably shaped by the archive: we begin by consulting catalog entries, finding aids, auction descriptions, and provenance records and by requesting permission to access the manuscript. In other words, we almost always view a literary manuscript in an institutional setting, having agreed to comply with protocols for viewing and handling it; within these settings, our access to and interactions with the manuscript are usually rigidly controlled. When a manuscript is presented to us, we also encounter the archival folders, custom-made cases, conservation bindings, and other supports used to house it, as well as notations or additional documents about the artifact itself. Manuscripts are often altered by the institution or by previous owners; they might have been disbound or rebound, stamped or conserved in ways that are less or more apparent, depending on our expertise and the records that have been made of these processes. All of these elements reflect the treatment of these manuscript objects over time and necessarily, if often invisibly, impact our understanding of them. These physical manifestations should not be regarded as impeding access to a more pure or original form of the manuscript, nor should we overlook them, as they can be examined for the evidence of the processes of acquisition, conservation, and use that are almost always embedded in a manuscript or its archival containers and institutional contexts.

In the past two decades, we have been able to interact with eighteenth-century literary manuscripts as digital surrogates, usually as digital photographic facsimiles that have been published online. Previous generations of scholars and students who wished to view a manuscript and could not access the original might have been able to consult microform and microfiche facsimiles or might have used print facsimiles, critical editions, or other scholarly and archival descriptions in an attempt to understand its textual and physical nature. As users of archives, print, and digital facsimiles, we ought to investigate what information about the physical object has been preserved and transmitted, and what information may have been lost, overlooked, obscured or withheld.

Beyond these physical manifestations of mediation, our relationship to historical manuscripts is usually impacted by other more intangible forces. Many literary manuscripts by well-known authors have acquired considerable economic value, having sold for amounts that would have been shocking to the original creators and the family members and literary associates who were their first conservators. The monetary value invested in these manuscripts has practical consequences: it affects how the manuscripts are treated by the institutions that have purchased them and the access those institutions provide. This consecration by the market also unquestionably impacts the perception of these manuscripts on the part of researchers and the general public. In addition, many scholars have theorized that a connection can be felt between an autograph manuscript and the physical body of the (long dead) author who created it, thus lending to all original artifacts what Walter Benjamin has described as an "aura," as the manuscript stands in for the body of the author.[97] This aura also presents another intangible layer of mediation to our interactions with manuscripts.

The economic, cultural, and affective capital that is invested in literary manuscripts of the long eighteenth century is to a degree arbitrary. Much depends, of course, on whether a literary manuscript survives in the first place, and there are strong reasons to believe that preservation practices were uneven, with authors who achieved celebrity in their own lifetimes being the most likely to have substantial archives. Some authors (generally male), like Samuel Richardson, Walter Scott, and William Wordsworth, preserved large quantities of their own manuscripts, while others who achieved early acclaim, like Alexander Pope and Thomas Gray, saw their correspondence and draft works avidly collected by their contemporaries. The survival of these manuscripts in turn catalyzes other forms of attention; in addition to interest on the part of collectors and institutions, their existence drives scholarly and technical innovation, in the form of critical editions and facsimiles, and, more recently, digital editions.

These forms of attention create new ways for students, scholars, and the general public to access manuscripts and acquire a better understanding of eighteenth-century literary culture, but this understanding is a selective one. There is an ever-present need to reflect critically on which literary manuscripts receive attention, and why. Beyond the trajectories of individual writing careers, scholars have increasingly become attentive to broader patterns of gaps and silences in the archive, recognizing that what survives is partial and incomplete and reflects power hierarchies and systemic forms of oppression. Given that literary creation requires access to literacy, education, and leisure, it is necessarily the case that literary manuscript culture was not equally available to all members of eighteenth-century society. At the same time, circulating one's writing in manuscript was often more accessible than print to those without connections, wealth, or power. In this way, efforts to locate and access less well-known manuscript sources that do survive, such as the poetry notebooks of Sarah Wilmot or of even more obscure authors of miscellanies and religious writing, can provide glimpses into worlds that are poorly represented in print culture.[98] Recent discoveries of manuscript verse by Phillis Wheatley and of almost fifty copiously annotated books and pamphlets belonging to the writer and philosopher Mary Astell remind us that the archive is not yet fully known.

---

[97] Benjamin, "Work."
[98] See Whelan, *Other British Voices*; Winckles, *Eighteenth-century Women's Writing*.

This section, and this Element more generally, is weighted toward well-known authors, in part because those are the manuscripts we have and the ones that have been studied. However, we also consider how recent developments in digital remediation generally, and more specifically in evolving institutional policies allowing readers to use digital photography and to publish those images, could be applied to great effect in recovering and making available the work of less well-known authors and manuscript creators. This section offers a set of strategies for identifying and interrogating any literary manuscript, returning to many of the cases discussed in the previous section as offering rich examples of analog and digital forms of remediation. "Remediation" is a term coined by Jay David Bolter and Richard Grusin to refer to how newer media forms inevitably incorporate older media; it also refers to how a work created for one medium (like a literary manuscript) is transformed for representation in a new medium (like a digital edition).[99] Attending to these material interventions helps us recover different practices of collection and preservation, understand the impact of these practices on our examination and interpretation of literary manuscripts, and theorize how shifting cultural conceptions of literary manuscripts impact our engagements with them today. Digital facsimiles in particular, which now provide unprecedented access to literary manuscripts, are often created to virtually reunify manuscripts that have been scattered to various institutions. At the same time, as the newest and perhaps least understood means of providing access, digital representations of literary manuscripts demand our scrutiny; we also need to ask which authors and which literary manuscripts become the subjects of digital remediations. Throughout, we suggest practical strategies for how to use these resources with care and skill while simultaneously asking, "what is it we can learn from these manuscripts?"

5.1 Archival Remediation

Acts of manuscript preservation may be deliberate or accidental, and often, as discussed in the previous section, we do not know precisely why a manuscript was retained in the first instance. With Laurence Sterne's first volume of *A Sentimental Journey*, we do know that at some point in the early decades of the nineteenth century it was acquired by the autograph collector William Upcott (1779–1845). Upcott made a career of collecting correspondence and literary manuscripts, as well as books, prints, and drawings, amassing an enormous collection: at his death on September 23, 1845, at the age of sixty-six, he possessed some 32,000 letters. Upcott is an important figure in the

---

[99] Bolter and Grusin, *Remediation*.

history of manuscript studies, as his self-described "disease" of "autographic mania" both initiates and reflects a larger cultural shift toward the collection of contemporary literary manuscripts.[100] What makes Upcott unique is that he was interested in the manuscripts of well-known authors, like Sterne, but also in those of lesser-known figures. As a librarian at the London Institute, Upcott could not afford to collect large numbers of documents of known historical or cultural value. He was able to acquire reams of correspondence primarily from his connections with publishers, who gave him authors' letters that they no longer needed and deemed to have no literary, cultural, or economic value. Upcott was ahead of his time in making the deliberate choice to preserve manuscripts not valued by anyone else, thus saving perhaps hundreds of letters and other literary manuscripts from destruction.

Upcott extra-illustrated the manuscript of *A Sentimental Journey*, a process of customization we saw with William Blake's copy of Thomas Gray's poems (see Figure 19); with Sterne's manuscript, Upcott added a handwritten title page (Figure 22), authenticating it as being "in the autograph of the Author," and bound the manuscript with other pieces of memorabilia, or "Sterneana," including engravings and letters. Notwithstanding Upcott's framing of the manuscript, the British Library website's page offers little description of Upcott's extra-illustration; similarly, the standard critical edition of the work makes no mention of Upcott by name, stating that the manuscript was bound with other materials "typical of a Victorian scrapbook on any subject."[101] Nevertheless, the Sterneana used to adorn the manuscript can tell us about the novelist's reception more than seven decades after the composition and publication of *A Sentimental Journey,* and about collection practices more generally.

Inscriptions, stamps, and extra-illustration, as well as other marks on manuscripts such as library plates and dedications, document not only provenance but also how a given manuscript was used and valued over time. With Sterne's manuscript, Upcott believed he was both preserving and enhancing its value by adding other Sterne-related material. Although Upcott did paste some of the illustrations to the blank versos of the manuscript (Sterne wrote only on the recto except in a few cases), it seems he was careful not to mark the manuscript itself. Indeed, the only marks visible are the stamps of the British Museum, in red ink, on many of the blank versos, though this stamp dates from between 1929 and 1973. The manuscript has affixed to it a letter from Jemima Day dated to 1843, suggesting that acquisition was probably shortly after that, perhaps upon Upcott's death in 1845, though the manuscript does not appear in the lengthy catalogs advertising the sale of Upcott's

---

[100] Upcott, "Autobiography," p. 476.   [101] Sterne, *Sentimental*, p. xxxvi.

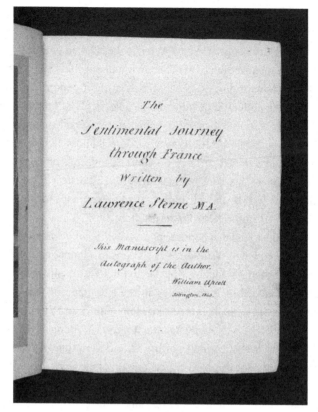

Figure 22 Sterne, Laurence. A Sentimental Journey Through France, 1768.
(British Library Egerton MS 1610).

collections. Although we do not know the circumstances by which Sterne's manuscript came to be saved in the first place, a careful examination of it reveals the many subsequent deliberate acts that led to it being preserved, embellished, and taken into an institutional collection.

Understanding how literary manuscripts bear the marks of their past circulation, ownership, and sale, as well as their changing market value, enables us to historicize how they were gifted and collected, bought and sold. This provenance is available in the case of Jane Austen's fiction manuscripts. As discussed in Section 4, we know that she was the first conservator of her own writing because she copied some (though not all) of her juvenile writing into the three notebooks that became Volume the First, Volume the Second, Volume the Third.[102] After Austen's death at the age of 41 in 1817, her sister Cassandra

---

[102] Sabor, *Juvenilia*, pp. xxix–xxxi.

inherited all of the manuscripts. Upon Cassandra's death in 1845, the manuscripts were bequeathed to various family members, and these family members, over the course of the next century, donated or sold the manuscripts to various institutions, the result being that now all of the surviving literary manuscripts are dispersed across institutions in the United Kingdom and the United States. Through this process, Austen's manuscripts changed form. The British Library, when it acquired Jane Austen's handmade manuscript notebooks of the canceled *Persuasion* chapters from her niece in 1925, had the leaves separated, trimmed, foliated, and mounted in a British Library bound volume. The unfinished draft of "The Watsons" has undergone a more startling transformation, and its story reveals the vagaries of manuscript survival. An initial division of the manuscript occurred when William Austen-Leigh, Jane and Cassandra Austen's grand-nephew, auctioned the first six leaves of the manuscript in support of a Red Cross charity sale at the beginning of World War I, in 1915, for £65; it was sold a few more times before being purchased by the Morgan Library, in New York City, where the fragment remains. The Red Cross stamp may be seen at the lower right side of the first page of this manuscript (Figure 23). Because Austen drafted into small handmade notebooks, the sale of the first quire did no physical damage to the manuscript itself, but it did mean that the manuscript as a whole was separated into parts, a practice that would likely not be condoned today, even in support of a good cause. The larger part of the manuscript passed from William Austen-Leigh to his descendants, who sold

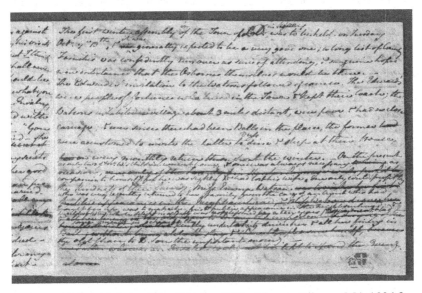

Figure 23 Jane Austen, "The Watsons," The Morgan Library. MA 1034.2

it in 1978 for £38,000 to the British Rail Pension Fund; then again in 1988 it was purchased at auction by Sir Peter Michael for £90,000. The manuscript was held on deposit at Queen Mary University; in 2005, during the process of digitization, the first four pages or "quire 2" went missing. A full investigation revealed no clues as to its disappearance. "The Watsons" is thus the only Austen manuscript in modern times to have been divided and partially lost, destroyed, or stolen. The remaining manuscript was put up for auction again in 2011 and, notwithstanding the valuation of £200,000–£300,000, it sold, after fierce bidding, for nearly £1,000,000, to the Bodleian Library. This history of auction values tracks the phenomenal increase not only in the market value of Austen's manuscripts but also of literary manuscripts generally.

As with the Red Cross charity stamp on the first page of "The Watsons," manuscripts can be inscribed with handwritten marks of ownership. Drafted on a single sheet, the recto of John Keats's draft of "To Autumn," dating from 1818, bears two inscriptions (Figure 24): (1) in the hand of Keats's brother, George: "Original manuscript of John Keats' poem to Autumn. Presented to Miss A Barker [later Ward] by the author's Brother," dated November 15, 1839 and (2) in a shakier hand, "Given to my granddaughter Elizabeth Ward May 14 '96. Anna H. B. Ward." Amy Lowell, the great collector of Keats, acquired the sheet from Ward in 1921 and bequeathed it to Harvard University Library in 1925. Thus, the manuscript, to borrow McGann's words, is "riven with the multiple histories of [its] own making"[103] and transmission: first by John Keats's drafting of the poem and sending it to his brother, subsequently by George Keats's presentation of and inscription on the draft to his friend Miss Barker, and later by Barker/Ward's presentation and inscription to her own granddaughter, thus documenting the passage of the manuscript over nearly a century. George Keats's handwritten inscription on the precious draft of one of his brother's most famous odes, as well as that added by Anna Barker/Ward, like the separation of "The Watsons," is a practice that would not be countenanced today. Still, the damage caused to this manuscript is far less egregious than that done by Keats's friend Charles Cowden Clarke to the draft of another Keats's poem, "I Stood Tiptoe on a little Hill," which Clarke cut into thirteen pieces to give to Keats's friends and admirers after the poet's death. Four of the thirteen fragments have never been traced, the locations of two additional fragments have been unknown since 1929, and six are in various institutions including the British Library, Houghton Library, Harvard, and the Scottish National Portrait Gallery. A final fragment of "I Stood Tiptoe" sold, in April 2013, for a staggering £181,250, four times the top estimate of £45,000; this and the

---

[103] McGann, *Republic*, p. 45.

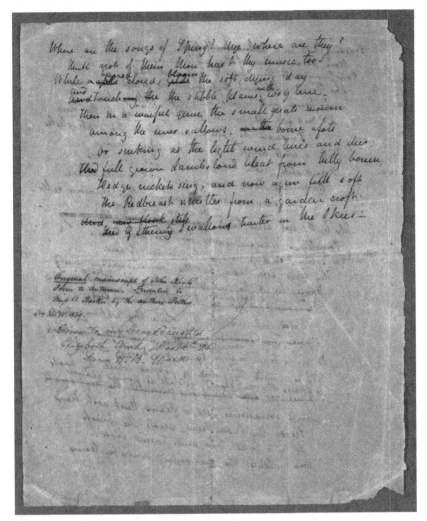

Figure 24 John Keats, "To Autumn" 1818. Houghton Library, Harvard University. MS Keats 2.27 A.MS

price fetched for Austen's "The Watsons" show that the value of literary manuscripts has never been higher.

5.2 Remediation beyond the Archive

After a literary manuscript had served its initial purpose, whether as a draft, a circulating copy, or a press copy or, as was often the case, some combination, its survival was usually the result of a conscious decision to preserve it, often for sentimental reasons – though occasionally, of course, manuscripts could survive due to benign neglect. At some point, however, they would pass to individuals who had no personal contact with the author but who nevertheless believed them worthy of saving. In relation to famous authors and well-known literary works, an interest often arose to see the manuscript. The purpose could be scholarly, as when editors wished to consult manuscripts to establish the text of a work, particularly if that work had not been printed. The handwriting of famous authors also held a fascination for the public; beginning in the eighteenth century, engraving was used to reproduce small segments of handwriting, such as a signature. Lithography, another reproductive technique, was developed in the early eighteenth century in part to enable the easier representation of handwriting in printed works. However, it was not until the development of photography, which promised a fidelity to the original that had not been possible in any previous copying technology, that handwriting, at least theoretically, could be more easily reproduced. Indeed, one of the earliest photographs ever made was of a literary manuscript, specifically of the last five lines of Lord Byron's "Ode to Napoleon," taken by one of the pioneers of photography, Henry Fox Talbot, in 1840.[104] Photography, however, remained expensive as a means of reproduction; as a result, few manuscripts were remediated this way in the nineteenth century. Nevertheless, as original manuscripts increasingly came to be preserved, collected, and archived, so too do we find the emergence of methods for reproducing all or parts of those manuscripts in other media forms, the process now commonly referred to as remediation.

In the early twentieth century, microphotography, which shrinks images to a fraction (1/25th or 4 percent) of their original size, was invented as a means of document preservation and dissemination. It came to be used in commercial and then in library/archival settings and was one of the primary ways in which twentieth-century scholars could engage with literary manuscripts. Unfortunately, photographic illustrations often reproduce poorly in microform format, with loss of clarity and halftones; these poor-quality images are often the source of digital collections, impeding research on literary manuscripts. Another way in which scholars could gain access to the textual content of literary manuscripts is through typed transcription. In Section 4, we surveyed two methods of transcription: diplomatic and what might be called a versioning method, which attempts to capture distinct textual versions or stages. However, as we saw, challenges attend attempting to reproduce even a very small excerpt from a draft manuscript. In part this is because most literary manuscripts are dynamic and do not follow the norms of type, which do not easily accommodate cancellations, interlinear and marginal notations, and other marks that are

---

[104] Burkett, "Photographing."

common in writing by hand. Within a manuscript, space, pages, and in the case of a notebook the binding itself can be used in a variety of ways. Writing can be multi-directional, and in different hands, inks, and sizes; it can be added over time, with some notebooks being used intergenerationally. Writing can be cancelled by striking through, erasing, blotting, cutting, or pasting over. All sorts of nonlinguistic shapes and drawings can appear on the page. Almost all of these marks are difficult if not impossible to reproduce in type. That is, even when a manuscript itself is perfectly legible, it is often impossible to translate its complexity into typed form; almost always something of the original is lost.

Charles Robinson's *The Frankenstein Notebooks* is a print facsimile that includes, on the verso, full-page images from the draft manuscript, and, on the facing page recto, a diplomatic transcription of the manuscript as well as a typed reproduction of the relevant sections of the first print edition. Robinson's print facsimile offers one of the finest examples of a scholarly transcription; he innovates in the use of italics to identify Percy Shelley's hand and to achieve accuracy in the placement of Shelley's interlinear and marginal revisions. At the same time, the facsimile also readily conveys the limits of print. In the printed reproduction of the manuscript page, the differences in ink tones are erased, and, as Robinson notes, "darker areas in photo-facsimile exaggerate curled paper at left edge as well as soiling and discoloration of paper."[105] The section of the manuscript transcribed earlier can be seen in the user interface of the *Shelley-Godwin Archive*, which uses Robinson's transcriptions but accompanied by far superior, high-quality color digital photographs of the manuscript's pages, images that would have been prohibitively expensive to reproduce in print. Whereas Robinson used fonts in his transcriptions to differentiate between Mary Shelley's and Percy Shelley's handwriting, the digital version allows its users to see the manuscript in diplomatic transcription or to select the handwriting of "Mary Shelley" or "Percy Shelley," in which case the handwriting of the unselected writer is greyed out.[106] The ability to toggle between the contributions of one or the other or both Shelleys is made possible because the marks made on the manuscript page have been encoded, meaning that the words (even individual letters) and punctuation have been carefully described and attributed to one or the other Shelley in computer code (here TEI-XML, which can be viewed by the user on the website). This textual encoding also enables a user of the digital archive to search within and across different manuscripts within the archive.

[105] Robinson, *Frankenstein*, p. 11n.
[106] http://shelleygodwinarchive.org/sc/oxford/ms_abinger/c56/#/p8.

Searchability is one of the primary ways in which a digitally encoded transcribed manuscript is different from a microform or print facsimile.

Digitizing manuscripts allows for precious original documents to be preserved and made accessible and, in the case of innovative encoding and display like the *Shelley-Godwin Archive*, it allows multiple types of interaction. The digital platform provides additional functionality: with high-quality images, it is possible to zoom in to observe exceptional detail or to rotate the manuscript and to switch between views, to see the manuscript image alone or alongside the transcription. Arrow bars allow one to move forward and backward in the manuscript page-by-page, and a vertical slider bar in the right margin shows where one is within a manuscript, with the slider bar enabling another way of moving quickly through the digitized manuscript pages. Many of these features allow one to view and manipulate a manuscript in ways that would be impossible even if permission were granted to view it in person. The other important feature of the *Shelley-Godwin Archive* is that because each page has its own digital photograph (and encoded transcription), it is possible to group the pages differently. This is important because, as discussed, Mary Shelley wrote the draft in notebooks that were disbound, possibly by her during the process of creating a fair copy. Currently the Bodleian Library divides the draft notebook pages into two discrete collections, MS Abinger c.56 and c.57, but this division does not align with the division in the original notebooks (A and B). It is possible within the digital realm to view the manuscript pages of the draft (1) in the physical sequence in which they are currently held in the Bodleian Library, MS Abinger c.56 and c.57,[107] or (2) as they would appear in virtually reconstituted Notebooks A and B (Notebook A contains all of MS Abinger c.56 and the first part of MS Abinger c.57; Notebook B contains the latter part of MS Abinger c.57).[108] Both of these presentations include extraneous fragments of another text that were included in the notebooks. One can also view the pages in (3) the linear chapter sequence of the two-notebook draft, which removes the fragments and organizes the pages into chapters.[109] However, as with older media forms, distortions can be created through the process of digitization. For example, manuscripts displayed on a screen almost always appear to be the same or nearly the same size. A ruler bar to the left in the *Shelley-Godwin Archive* page display seeks to provide this important context, but it cannot replicate the perception of size and dimensionality that arises from viewing

---

[107] http://shelleygodwinarchive.org/contents/ms_abinger_c56/ and http://shelleygodwinarchive .org/contents/ms_abinger_c57/

[108] http://shelleygodwinarchive.org/contents/frankenstein_notebook_a/ and http://shelleygodwi narchive.org/contents/frankenstein_notebook_b/

[109] http://shelleygodwinarchive.org/contents/frankenstein/#oxford_frankenstein_volume_i

and handling a manuscript in person. Other aspects of the original cannot be easily reproduced: even the best zoom functionality cannot allow one to deduce the quality of the paper, its watermarks, its smoothness or thickness.

Because the notebooks of the draft and fair copies of *Frankenstein* have been disbound, the extant manuscripts of the novel do not face the greater challenges that emerge in seeking to display a work that is bound in a notebook. Photographing and digitally rendering pages from a three-dimensional book object present even greater difficulties; a variety of options exist for its digital representation, and choices and often trade-offs must be made. The challenge of representing a codex is addressed in the three user interfaces that display Jane Austen's juvenile "History of England," from Volume the Second. The first, provided by *Jane Austen's Fiction Manuscripts*, a digital edition of Austen's extant fiction manuscripts providing full diplomatic transcriptions, digitally cuts the notebook layout along the spine, near the gutter, presenting each page image separately.[110] The imaging is done sensitively, such that a small slice of the facing page is visible, confirming that the page we are viewing is bound within a notebook. Given that the edition includes diplomatic transcriptions, and the aim is to present these alongside the manuscript page images, this choice makes sense. However, we are unable to visualize other aspects of the notebook, such as the spine, and it is difficult to tell if pages have been cut out (creating stubs).

The British Library, the owner of Volume the Second, displays "The History of England" in two user interfaces on its website. Both display the recto and verso, representing how the notebook is viewed when held open. One user interface allows the manuscript notebook to be viewed with the proprietary software Turning the Pages, which allows users to simulate, within a digital facsimile, the turning of a page, whether by moving a cursor or, with a touch screen, using their fingers to do so.[111] By curling back a page, one is able simultaneously to see part of the recto and verso of a single leaf, a fascinating approximation of three dimensionality. Viewing Austen's "The History of England" within Turning the Pages, however, is in one respect misleading, as turning the page from the cover takes one immediately to "The History," even though it begins on page 153 of the notebook. "The History" can also be accessed in the British Library's Collection viewer, which likewise starts in the middle of the notebook, at the start of "The History," though this presentation is less deceptive as we do not open from the front cover immediately to page 153.[112] This British Library interface allows for remarkably crisp viewing

---

[110] *Jane Austen Fiction Manuscripts*, Ed. Kathryn Sutherland, https://janeausten.ac.uk/manuscripts/blvolsecond/171.html

[111] Navigate to www.bl.uk/turning-the-pages/ and search for "Jane Austen History of England."

[112] www.bl.uk/collection-items/history-of-england-austen-juvenilia#

and also displays a transcription, in a pop-up box, if that option is selected. Both viewers, while representing the physicality of the notebook, nevertheless separate "The History" from the many pieces that come before and after in the notebook Austen designated as Volume the Second. In seeking to showcase "The History," the British Library digitally severs it from the rest of the notebook's contents, while adopting an opening layout view does capture its placement within a bound notebook. *Jane Austen's Fiction Manuscripts*, as we have seen, makes a different choice, forgoing the opening or layout view and the perception of the notebook to accommodate the presentation of transcriptions. By including photofacsimiles and transcriptions of all pages within the notebook, it also calls attention to the relation of "The History" to the other contents of the notebook. Indeed, it is impossible to navigate directly to "The History" within the notebook unless one happens to know on what page it appears.

Digital media have revolutionized access to literary manuscripts. Online collections like *Jane Austen's Fiction Manuscripts* and the *Shelley-Godwin Archive* digitally reunify the literary manuscripts of writers that are currently held in different institutional repositories, sometimes on different continents, enabling comparisons at the click of a button that do not endanger the original documents. Of course, we should also be cognizant that the investment made in digital editions is significant and that by and large it has been the well-known authors who have been favored with the greatest attention (the three online versions of Jane Austen's "The History of England" are a case in point). Further, we should remain attuned to the losses involved in working with digital copies, to what they cannot replicate, and what they can distort. However, the ability of researchers to use digital photography in archives, a practice that is increasingly allowed and even encouraged, and the willingness of many archives to photograph and make widely available digital images of their manuscript holdings, can serve as a remarkable aid to research and teaching, one that promises to unlock the archive in ways that were unimaginable just a few short decades ago.

Coda: Loss, Discovery, and the Importance of Manuscript Studies

On February 10, 1785, the following advertisement appeared in a Boston newspaper:

> The person who borrowed a volume of manuscript poems && of Phillis Peters, formerly Phillis Wheatley, deceased, would very much oblige her husband, John Peters, by returning it immediately, as the whole of her works are intended to be published.[1]

This borrowed volume of manuscript poems, which included a selection of letters (the "&&"), while it may have been recovered by John Peters, has since been lost without a trace.[2] We can identify its probable contents, however, in the form of two proposals for the planned subscription publication, which would have been Wheatley's second book, that appeared in Boston periodicals in 1779 and 1784. Phillis Wheatley thus offers a potent concluding reminder that few authors in the eighteenth century circulated their work exclusively in either manuscript or print, and that scholars of eighteenth-century literary culture must be prepared to engage with both media. Wheatley's career also demonstrates that movement between scribal and print publication is never assured, seldom straightforward, and often subject to loss in the process. Of Wheatley's fifty-seven known poems, forty-six were published in print during her lifetime. Nine were published in magazines and broadsides before her printed poetry collection, *Poems on Various Subjects, Religious and Moral*, appeared in London in September 1773; the volume included thirty-nine poems, of which five had been previously published; three additional poems appeared in broadsides and magazines between 1773 and her death in 1784. Her second volume of poems and letters never appeared in print even though it was advertised for five years, defying critical assumptions that once a writer has printed her work, she will inevitably continue to do so. Eleven poems survive only in manuscript versions, twenty-three poems are known only by their titles in the 1779 and 1784 proposals, and almost certainly more have been lost.[3]

However, there is reason to hope that more of Wheatley's writing may be recovered. In 2009, in the back cover of the 1773 diary of the Rev. Jeremy Belknap (a diary that itself is interleaved in a printed almanac), Vincent Carretta found a poem Belknap titled "Phillis Wheatley's first Effort – AD 1765. AE 11

---

[1] Caretta, *Phillis*, p. 190. [2] Dayton, "Lost Years," 351, n.98.
[3] Caretta, *Writings*, pp. xxxvii; 137–39; 143; 212–3.

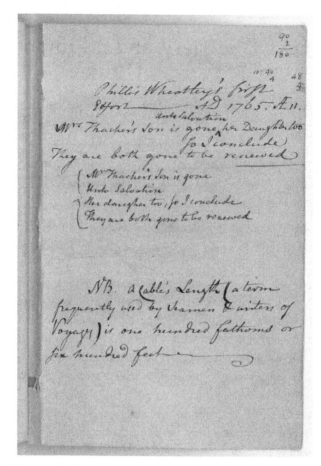

Figure 25 Jeremy Belknap, Diary. 1773. MS N-1827. Jeremy Belknap Papers, Diaries 1758–1798. Massachusetts Hist. Soc., Boston.

[Age 11]" (Figure 25). Written four years after Wheatley was abducted as a child from the Senegambia region of Africa, enslaved, and brought to Boston, this poem was discovered through the collaboration of Carretta's diligent scholarship, archivists' assistance, and Belknap's transcription of the poem eight years after it was written in 1773. In 1791, Belknap founded the Massachusetts Historical Society, where his diary is preserved. Such discoveries are also possible because of the durability of eighteenth-century paper, ink, and the stiffened boards used in bookbinding.

The creation, circulation, and preservation of Phillis Wheatley's poetic manuscripts was at once utterly commonplace – practiced by many of her era, as this Element has shown – and entirely extraordinary. Although the early compositions of precocious children were regularly copied and saved,

Belknap's attention to Wheatley's "first Effort," which he transcribes twice, on two separate occasions as we can tell from the change in ink, was in all likelihood due to her status as an enslaved person. Wheatley's exceptionality inevitably heightened interest in her verse; at the same time, the novelty was not sufficient to ensure the publication of her second volume of poems, or the survival of most of them in manuscript. While Wheatley's heartbreakingly incomplete story amplifies our awareness of the silences of the archive, it also has much to tell us about the potential of manuscript study to expand our knowledge of literary culture in the eighteenth century, particularly where status and circumstances have constrained access to print.

This Element has been written entirely during the global pandemic of 2020–21, a period that has reminded us, more viscerally than perhaps any other single event in many of our lifetimes, of what the historical archive can tell us about the aspirations of humanity. In our reading of the literary manuscripts of the eighteenth century, we find the profound desire for human sociability, for expression and connection, constantly on display, even among those without full human rights and freedoms. The fundamentally sociable nature of literary culture is reflected in the drafting and sharing of poetry, correspondence, journals, and fiction; in the collaborative production of verse and prose; in the negotiation between intimately known and wider, anonymous audiences; in the painstaking transfer of texts from one medium to another; in the collecting and arrangement of literary writing; and in the preservation and gifting of manuscripts themselves. We remain thankful for the earliest preservers of the literary manuscripts we study today for their stewardship of the historical record and are immensely grateful to the curators, archivists, and librarians who continue to care for these documents. We appreciate the many good-natured responses to our queries about archival holdings during this difficult period; our project would have been impossible without such support. Nor could we have completed this Element without relying on digitized manuscripts and digital editions, which provide access to historical documents in ways that previous generations could have only imagined. We are indebted to the scholars, librarians, and technology experts who have created these resources, and who pour their time and energy into their maintenance and improvement. As we look forward to archives opening up in the coming year, we remain convinced that there has never been a better or more urgent time to roll up our sleeves and get to work, to discover and rediscover what we can learn from the period's manuscript record.

References

Allan, David. *Commonplace Books and Reading in Georgian England.* Cambridge: Cambridge University Press, 2010.

Astell, Mary, and John Norris. *Letters Concerning the Love of God.* London, 1705.

Austen, Henry. "Biographical Notice of the Author." In *Northanger Abbey: and Persuasion.* London, 1818.

Austen-Leigh, James Edward *A Memoir of Jane Austen: Second Edition.* London: Bentley, 1871.

Bannet, Eve Tavor. *Empire of Letters: Letter Manuals and Transatlantic Correspondence, 1680–1820.* Cambridge: Cambridge University Press, 2005.

Beal, Peter. *A Dictionary of English Manuscript Terminology 1450–2000.* Oxford: Oxford University Press, 2008.

"Notions in Garrison: The Seventeenth-Century Commonplace Book." In *New Ways of Looking at Old Texts: Papers of the Renaissance English Text Society, 1985–1991*, edited by W. Speed Hill, 131–47. Binghamton, NY: Center for Medieval and Early Renaissance Studies, 1993.

Benjamin, Walter. "The Work of Art in the Age of Mechanical Reproduction." In *Illuminations*, edited by Hannah Arendt, 217–51. New York: Schocken, 1969.

Bigold, Melanie. *Women of Letters, Manuscript Circulation, and Print Afterlives in the Eighteenth Century: Elizabeth Rowe, Catharine Cockburn and Elizabeth Carter.* London: Palgrave Macmillan, 2013.

Bland, Mark. *A Guide to Early Printed Books and Manuscripts.* Malden, MA: Blackwell, 2013.

Bolter, Jay David and Richard Grusin. *Remediation: Understanding New Media.* Cambridge, MA: MIT Press, 1999.

Burkett, Andrew. "Photographing Byron's Hand." *European Romantic Review* 26, no. 2 (2005): 129–48.

Carretta, Vincent. *Phillis Wheatley: Biography of a Genius in Bondage.* Athens: University of Georgia Press, 2011.

ed. *The Writings of Phillis Wheatley.* Oxford: Oxford University Press, 2019.

Chalus, Elaine. *Elite Women in English Political Life, c. 1754–1790.* Oxford: Clarendon Press, 2005.

Colclough, Stephen. *Consuming Texts: Readers and Reading Communities, 1697–1890.* New York: Palgrave Macmillan, 2007.

Curran, Louise. *Samuel Richardson and the Art of Letter-Writing*. Cambridge: Cambridge University Press, 2016.

Daybell, James. *The Material Letter in Early Modern England: Manuscript Letters and the Culture and Practices of Letter-Writing, 1512–1635*. London: Palgrave Macmillan, 2012.

Dayton, Cornelia H. "Lost Years Recovered John Peters and Phillis Wheatley Peters in Middleton." *The New England Quarterly* 94 (2021): 309–51.

Eger, Elizabeth. *Bluestockings: Women of Reason from Enlightenment to Romanticism*. London: Palgrave Macmillan, 2010.

Ellis, Markman. "*The English Mercurie* Hoax and the Early History of the Newspaper." *Book History* 22 (2019): 100–32.

"Letters, Organization, and the Archive in Elizabeth Montagu's Correspondence," edited by Nicole Pohl. Special issue, *The Huntington Library Quarterly* 81, no. 4 (2018): 603–31.

"Thomas Birch's 'Weekly Letter' (1741–66): Correspondence and History in the Mid-Eighteenth-Century Royal Society." *Notes & Records* 68 (2014): 261–78.

Ezell, Margaret J. M. "Invisible Books." In *Producing the Eighteenth-Century Book: Writers and Publishers in England, 1650–1800*, edited by Laura L. Runge and Pat Rogers, 53–69. Newark: University of Delaware Press, 2009.

Social Authorship and the Advent of Print. Baltimore, MD: Johns Hopkins University Press, 1999.

Garrick, David. *The Private Correspondence of David Garrick*. 2 vols. Edited by James Boaden. London: Henry Colburn and Richard Bentley, 1831.

Gray, Thomas. *An Elegy wrote in a Country Church Yard*. London, 1751.

Guest, Harriet. *Small Change: Women, Learning, Patriotism, 1750–1810*. Chicago: University of Chicago Press, 2000.

Gunther, Albert Everard. *An Introduction to the Life of the Rev. Thomas Birch D.D., F.R.S. 1705–1766*. Halesworth, UK: Halesworth, 1984.

Havens, Hilary. *Revising the Eighteenth-Century Novel: Authorship from Manuscript to Print*. Cambridge: Cambridge University Press, 2019.

Heller, Deborah. "The Bluestockings and Virtue Friendship: Elizabeth Montagu, Anne Pitt, and Elizabeth Carter," edited by Nicole Pohl. Special issue, *The Huntington Library Quarterly* 81, no. 4 (2018): 469–96.

Hobbs, Mary. *Early Seventeenth-Century Verse Miscellany Manuscripts*. Aldershot, UK: Scolar Press, 1992.

James, Kathryn. *English Paleography and Manuscript Culture, 1500–1800*. New Haven, CT: Yale University Press, 2000.

Justice, George, and Nathan Tinker, eds. *Women's Writing and the Circulation of Ideas: Manuscript Publication in England, 1550–1800*. Cambridge and New York: Cambridge University Press, 2002.

Keown, Kathleen. "Eighteenth-Century Women's Poetry and the Feminine Accomplishment." *Review of English Studies*, New Series, 1–22. doi: 10.1093/res/hgab033.

Keymer, Thomas, and Peter Sabor, eds. "General Editors' Preface." In *The Cambridge Edition of the Correspondence of Samuel Richardson*. Cambridge: Cambridge University Press, 2013–. 1.ix–xxii.

King, Rachael Scarborough. *After Print. Eighteenth-Century Manuscript Cultures*. Charlottesville: University of Virginia Press, 2020.

Writing to the World: Letters and the Origins of Modern Print Genres. Baltimore, MD: Johns Hopkins University Press, 2018.

Levy, Michelle. *Family Authorship and Romantic Print Culture*. Basingstoke, UK: Palgrave, 2008.

Literary Manuscript Culture in Romantic Britain. Edinburgh: Edinburgh University Press, 2020.

"Women and the Book in Britain's Long Eighteenth Century." *Literature Compass* 17, no. 9 (2020): 1–3.

Love, Harold. *The Culture and Commerce of Texts: Scribal Publication in Seventeenth-Century England*. Oxford: Clarendon Press, 1998.

Scribal Publication in Seventeenth-Century England. Oxford: Clarendon, 1993.

McCarthy, William, ed. *The Collected Works of Anna Letitia Barbauld. The Poems, Revised*. Oxford: Oxford University Press, 2019.

"What Did Anna Barbauld Do to Samuel Richardson's Correspondence? A Study of Her Editing." *Studies in Bibliography* 54 (2001): 191–223.

Marotti, Arthur F. *Manuscript, Print, and the English Renaissance Lyric*. Ithaca, NY: Cornell University Press, 1995.

McGann, Jerome. *A New Republic of Letters: Memory and Scholarship in the Age of Digital Reproduction*. Cambridge, MA: Harvard University Press, 2014.

McKitterick, David. *Print, Manuscript and the Search for Order 1450–1830*. Cambridge and New York: Cambridge University Press, 2003.

Mellor, Anne K. *Mary Shelley, Her Life, Her Fiction, Her Monsters*. New York: Methuen, 1988.

Montagu, Elizabeth. *The Letters of Mrs. Elizabeth Montagu, with Some Letters of her Correspondence*. 4 vols. Edited by Matthew Montagu. London, 1809–13.

Myers, Sylvia Harcstark. *The Bluestocking Circle: Women, Friendship, and the Life of the Mind in Eighteenth-Century England*. Oxford: Clarendon, 1990.

Orchard, Jack. "Dr. Johnson on Trial: Catherine Talbot and Jemima Grey Responding to Samuel Johnsons's *The Rambler.*" *Women's Writing* 23 (2016): 193–210.

Paul, Zoe. "Comparing Mrs. Wilmot's 'To Harry at Eton' and 'From Mrs. Wilmot to Her Daughter.' *Sarah Wilmot, Forgotten Bluestocking* (blog). https://sarahwilmot.omeka.net/exhibits/show/harry-at-eton-and-to -her-daugh/analysis-essay-paul.

Pickering, Oliver. "The BCMSV Database: A Progress Report and a Case Story." *Library Review* 44, no. 3 (1995): 24–31.

Reiman, Donald H. *The Study of Modern Manuscripts: Public, Confidential, and Private.* Baltimore, MD: Johns Hopkins University Press, 1993.

Robinson, Charles E., ed. *The Frankenstein Notebooks.* London: Garland, 1996.

Sabor, Peter, ed. *The Cambridge Edition of the Works of Jane Austen: Juvenilia.* Cambridge: Cambridge University Press, 2013.

Schellenberg, Betty A. "Catherine Talbot Translates Samuel Richardson: Bridging Social Networks and Media Cultures in the Mid-Eighteenth Century." *Eighteenth-Century Fiction* 29 (2016–17): 201–20.

"Eighteenth-Century Manuscript Verse Miscellanies and the Print-Manuscript Interface," edited by Schellenberg and Michelle Levy. Special issue, *The Huntington Library Quarterly* 84, no. 1 (2021): 151–64.

Literary Coteries and the Making of Modern Print Culture 1740–1790. Cambridge: Cambridge University Press, 2016.

and Michelle Levy, eds. "Women in Book History, 1660–1830." Special issue, *The Huntington Library Quarterly* 84, no. 1 (2021).

Stallybrass, Peter. "Printing and the Manuscript Revolution." In *Explorations in Communication and History,* edited by Barbie Zelizer, 111–18. New York: Routledge, 2008.

Sterne, Laurence. *A Sentimental Journey through France and Italy and Continuation of the Bramine's Journal. The text and notes.* Edited by Melvyn New and W. G. Day. Gainesville: University of Florida Press, 2002.

Trolander, Paul, and Zenep Tenger. *Sociable Criticism in England 1625–1725.* Newark: University of Delaware Press, 2007.

Upcott, William. "Autobiography of a Collector." *Gentleman's Magazine.* 2nd ser. 25 (May 1846): 474–76.

Whelan, Timothy. *Other British Voices: Women, Poetry, and Religion, 1766–1840.* New York: Palgrave Macmillan, 2015.

Whyman Susan E. *The Pen and the People: English Letter Writers 1660–1800.* Oxford: Oxford University Press, 2009.

Williams, Abigail. *The Social Life of Books: Reading Together in the Eighteenth-Century Home*. New Haven, CT: Yale University Press, 2017.

Winckles, Andrew O. *Eighteenth-Century Women's Writing and the Methodist Media Revolution: "Consider the Lord as Ever Present Reader."* Liverpool: Liverpool University Press, 2019.

Wolfe, Heather. "Was Early Modern Writing Paper Expensive?" *The Collation: Research and Exploration at the Folger* (Feb. 13, 2018). https://collation .folger.edu/2018/02/writing-paper-expensive/.

Wordsworth, William. "Preface to Lyrical Ballads, 1800." In *Lyrical Ballads and Other Poems*. Ithaca: Cornell University Press, 1992.

Manuscripts Referenced

Blake, William. *Illustrations to Poems of Mr Gray*. 1797–98. www .blakearchive.org/copy/but335.1?descId=but335.1.wc.01

Sutherland, Kathryn, ed. *Jane Austen's Fiction Manuscripts: A Digital Edition*. 2010. www.janeausten.ac.uk.

Austen, Cassandra. "Memorandum." Morgan Library, MA 2911.1.

Austen, Jane. "History of England." Volume the Second. *Jane Austen Fiction Manuscripts*, edited by Kathryn Sutherland. janeausten.ac.uk/manu scripts/blvolsecond/171.html

"History of England." Volume the Second. c. 1790–1793. www.bl.uk/collec tion-items/volume-the-second-austen-juvenilia

Persuasion. 1818. British Library, Egerton MS 3038. www.bl.uk/collection-items/manuscript-of-chapters-10-and-11-from-jane-austens-persuasion

"The Watsons." c. 1805. The Morgan Library. MA 1034.2. www .themorgan.org/literary-historical/81930.

Barbauld, Anna. "To a little invisible being who is expected soon to become visible." *Miscellaneous Extracts*. Private Collection, William McCarthy.

Forster Collection, MSS. XI–XVI [Samuel Richardson's Correspondence]. National Art Library, Victoria and Albert Museum, London, UK.

Gray, Thomas. "Elegy in a Country Churchyard." www.thomasgray.org/

Grey, Jemima. "Letters to Catherine Talbot." Bedfordshire and Luton Archives and Records Service, Lucas Papers, L9a.

Hardwicke Papers, Vol L, *Correspondence of Philip Yorke, 2nd Earl of Hardwicke, with Rev. Thomas Birch, D. D. Secretary to the Royal Society, joint author with Lord Hardwicke and others of the Athenian Letters (1741–1743), 1740–1766*. British Library Add MS 35396–35400.

Huber, Alexander, ed. "Finding Aid Results." *Thomas Gray Archive*, 02 Dec 2020. Web. 17 Mar 2021. www.thomasgray.org/cgi-bin/findaid.cgi? ead=grayt.ead.0001&collection=poems&work=elcc<color_White≫

Keats, John. "To Autumn." 1818. Houghton Library, Harvard University, MS Keats 2.27 A.MS. https://id.lib.harvard.edu/ead/d/8559b7ac-71ca-4287-8a65-014ebcdc64e3/catalog

Poems by John Keats. Transcribed by George Keats. British Library Egerton MS 2780. F.58v

Montagu Collection. The Huntington Library, San Marino, California.

Murray, John. Ledger of Rejected Manuscripts, National Library of Scotland, MS 42632.

Pope, Alexander. *The Iliad*, Letter to John Caryll. The British Library, BL MS Add. MS 4807.

Shelley, Mary, and Percy. *Frankenstein; or, the Modern Prometheus*. Bodleian Library, University of Oxford, MS Abinger c.56. http://shelleygodwinarc hive.org/contents/ms_abinger_c56/

Sterne, Lawrence. *A Sentimental Journey Through France*. 1768. British Library Egerton MS 1610. www.bl.uk/collection-items/laurence-sternes-manuscript-draft-of-the-first-part-of-a-sentimental-journey.

Talbot, Catherine. "Wrest Journal." Lucas Papers L30/106. Bedfordshire and Luton Archives and Records Service.

Wheatley, Phillis. "Phillis Wheatley's first Effort – AD 1765. AE 11." Jeremy Belknap, Diary. 1773. *Jeremy Belknap Papers, Diaries 1758–1798*. Massachusetts Hist. Soc., Boston. MS N-1827.

Wilmot, Elizabeth Sarah, "Three Manuscript Notebooks of Verse." 4946 WIL. Chawton House Library, Hampshire, UK.

"Wilmot and Garrick Upon Lord Camden's taking the Great Seal." Folger Shakespeare Library MS Y.1089, No. 10.

Wordsworth, Dorothy. "Lines intended for my Niece's Album." 1832. Commonplace Book. Wordsworth Trust, Dove Cottage Manuscript [DCMS] 120.

Acknowledgments

We wish to thank all those who have contributed their hard work and expertise to the preparation of this book. Research assistant Angela Wachowich verified facts. Editorial assistant Sara Penn pruned and corrected and formatted – the finished product is much the better for her watchful care. Darren Bevin and now Emma Yandle of the Chawton House Library, Jeff Cowton of the Wordsworth Trust, Elizabeth Denlinger of the New York Public Library, Markman Ellis of Queen Mary University of London, Jack Orchard of the Elizabeth Montagu Correspondence Online project, and Heather Wolfe of the Folger Shakespeare Library lent valuable assistance with regard to the manuscript collections we have drawn on as our case studies.

Eve Tavor Bannet and Rebecca Bullard, general editors of the Eighteenth-Century Connections series, together with Bethany Thomas and Adam Hooper of Cambridge University Press, provided the enthusiasm that launched this project and the useful direction that steered it safely home. We are grateful as well to the anonymous readers for the press whose feedback was both encouraging and valuable in the revision stages. We sincerely appreciate also the expert production work of Aloysias Thomas and his team at Integra Software Services. The Social Sciences and Humanities Research Council of Canada funded much of the research represented in this book, as well as the Women in Book History 1660–1830 Symposium that initiated our scholarly partnership. To our colleagues of the Women in Book History Symposium, as well as those in our eighteenth-century work-in-progress group at Simon Fraser University (SFU), we owe our thanks for contributing immeasurably to the sense of purpose behind this project.

Alison Moore on behalf of the SFU Library provided crucial Open Access funding, for which we are deeply grateful. It is only fitting that we conclude by thanking the owners, curators, archivists, editors, and web developers who have cared for eighteenth-century literary manuscripts over the generations and who continue to find new ways to make them accessible for our pleasure and study.

Cambridge Elements ⸗

Eighteenth-Century Connections

Series Editors

Eve Tavor Bannet
University of Oklahoma

Eve Tavor Bannet is George Lynn Cross Professor Emeritus, University of Oklahoma and editor of *Studies in Eighteenth-Century Culture*. Her monographs include *Empire of Letters: Letter Manuals and Transatlantic Correspondence 1688–1820* (Cambridge, 2005), *Transatlantic Stories and the History of Reading, 1720–1820* (Cambridge, 2011), and *Eighteenth-Century Manners of Reading: Print Culture and Popular Instruction in the Anglophone Atlantic World* (Cambridge, 2017). She is editor of *British and American Letter Manuals 1680–1810* (Pickering & Chatto, 2008), *Emma Corbett* (Broadview, 2011) and, with Susan Manning, *Transatlantic Literary Studies* (Cambridge, 2012).

Rebecca Bullard
University of Reading

Rebecca Bullard is Associate Professor of English Literature at the University of Reading. She is the author of *The Politics of Disclosure: Secret History Narratives, 1674–1725* (Pickering & Chatto, 2009), co-editor of *The Plays and Poems of Nicholas Rowe, volume 1* (Routledge, 2017) and co-editor of *The Secret History in Literature, 1660–1820* (Cambridge, 2017).

Advisory Board

Linda Bree, Independent
Claire Connolly, University College Cork
Gillian Dow, University of Southampton
James Harris, University of St Andrews
Thomas Keymer, University of Toronto
Jon Mee, University of York
Carla Mulford, Penn State University
Nicola Parsons, University of Sydney
Manushag Powell, Purdue University
Robbie Richardson, University of Kent
Shef Rogers, University of Otago
Eleanor Shevlin, West Chester University
David Taylor, Oxford University
Chloe Wigston Smith, University of York
Roxann Wheeler, Ohio State University
Eugenia Zuroski, MacMaster University

About the Series

Exploring connections between verbal and visual texts and the people, networks, cultures and places that engendered and enjoyed them during the long Eighteenth Century, this innovative series also examines the period's uses of oral, written and visual media, and experiments with the digital platform to facilitate communication of original scholarship with both colleagues and students.

Cambridge Elements ☰

Eighteenth-Century Connections

Elements in the Series

A full series listing is available at: www.cambridge.org/EECC